ROUTEMA
H

Third Edition

Andrew Morgan

Capital Transport

ISBN 185414 237 2

Published by
Capital Transport
Publishing
38 Long Elmes,
Harrow Weald,
Middlesex

Designed by
Tim Demuth

Printed by
CS Graphics, Singapore

© Andrew Morgan 2001

Third edition

Title page **RM 1425 has had its lower deck converted to a snack bar in St Etienne in France.** Danny Chabaud

Right **RM 2186 was one of the vehicles withdrawn by London Northern when route 139 was converted to one-person operation with low floor Dennis Darts in March 1998. It is now used in connection with the Tuxedo Princess nightclub under the famous Tyne Bridge at Gateshead.** Steven Oliver

I must thank the help and assistance of people too numerous to individually mention, but in particular Maurice Bateman and Keith Hamer. Additionally, this book would not have been possible without the continual patience of my wife and family. This publication is believed to be as accurate and up-to-date as possible and readers can keep this book up-to-date by consulting the news sheets of the London Omnibus Traction Society, the PSV Circle or the Routemaster Association.

Andrew Morgan
St Albans, December 2000.

CONTENTS

The Routemaster was the last bus to be wholly designed by London Transport for use in the capital. It was designed in the 1950s for the large scale replacement of the London trolleybus fleet. Although it is well known that the Routemaster was more expensive than alternative vehicles available at the time, it proved to be a vehicle with untouchable longevity. Some

RM 1005 and RM 1933 are seen in August 2000 at Trowell services on the M1 Motorway *en route* from PVS at Barnsley being returned to London for further use by London Bus Services Tony Potter

thought as the last vehicle entered service that the Routemaster design was obsolete, having been effectively killed off by its exclusion from 1960s Bus Grant Specifications. No one would have thought that hundreds of Routemasters would still be in use at the start of the 21st Century.

It is nearly twenty years since the first large scale withdrawals and sales of Routemasters by London Transport commenced. With the sudden emergence of large numbers of well maintained second-hand vehicles, the Routemaster was to be an obvious choice for would-be owners. But it was with the arrival of Deregulation from 1986, that the Routemaster proved to be a very useful tool in the highly competitive environment, and had the advantage over more modern vehicles of speed of loading and passenger acceptability. Hence large numbers of Routemasters left London for all over Britain. Although all major operations of Routemasters have been discontinued for one reason or another, the Routemaster continues to have its role to play in bus operation. Nowhere more so than the crowded streets of London, the home of the Routemaster. With the completion of the first round of the tendering of the crew routes in London, these operations are currently stable until the second round of tendering for the contracts for the various London Bus Services routes are renewed between the provisional dates of 2001 and 2006. From 3rd July 2000, Ken Livingstone, the new Mayor for London, took office and what was previously known as London Transport Buses became the responsibility of Transport for London under the leadership of the Mayor. He is known to support the use of conductors on buses, and supports the continued use of the Routemaster fleet for the foreseeable future.

As with other classes of London bus, examples have joined the ranks of preserved vehicles as well as the fleets of miscellaneous vehicles on non-psv duties. Also Routemasters of all varieties, including Airways and Northern General vehicles, have been exported and can be seen in at least 47 countries around the world for just about every conceivable use.

The early Routemasters have now been in psv service for longer than any RT class vehicle, and unless there is a dramatic change of policy, the

Former Kelvin RM 388 was rebuilt with an open staircase for Yorkshire Belles and was used on a sightseeing tour of York. Malcolm King

Routemaster should continue to see service until at least 2006. This is despite the fact that Routemaster vehicles are between 32 and 42 years old, yet were only built for a 15 year life span!

All Routemasters in London have, since 1996, used the so-called green ultra low sulphur fuel and from 1997, most have been fitted with particulate filters to their exhausts.

All routes re-tendered since the last edition of this book (September 1996) have been retained with continued operation with Routemaster vehicles, except London Northern route 139, which was converted to low floor Dennis Dart operation in March 1998. All surplus RMs from this route were quickly sold and again most went to dealers for re-sale, mostly to buyers abroad. With each tender announcement, it has become noteworthy that often the number of crew vehicles required has actually increased as the proposed frequency required by London Transport Buses has increased. Hence over this period, the number of surplus Routemasters available for service has diminished, accident damaged vehicles are usually repaired, often at any cost, and the refurbishment of RMs has taken place.

Reading Mainline was the last sizeable Routemaster operator outside London; it commenced operations on 23rd July 1994 and operated its last Routemaster six years later. In total, forty-three vehicles were acquired for operation including many vehicles from other operators around the British Isles as well as a few former preserved examples. The last vehicles acquired were the complete batch of twelve Leyland engined RMs from Blackpool Transport in early 1997, having last been operated by this company in September 1996. The operation was sold to Reading Buses on 2nd June 1998 with the condition of continued operation for a further two years; in actual fact this lasted two years and one month! The final day of operation was 22nd July 2000, when only Lines D and F were still run and a total of eleven RMs were available for operation.

Black Prince had operated RMs since September 1990 but acquired further RMs with two former United Counties RMs for operation on Leeds University route 63B from 9th December 1996. This operation continued until withdrawal in February 1998.

Another operator to commence operations with a great deal of optimism was Watford & District, which started operations in February 1997 when the former Timebus routes were taken over, but it lasted only seventeen days before ceasing operations. Three former Bournemouth RMs were acquired by this operator but in the end were not used in service. They were repainted in a livery of green, cream and silver which was very similar to the 1935 Maidstone and District livery.

The sightseeing operations of Blue Triangle were acquired by London Coaches in March 1997. Subsequently most sales of London Coaches RMs and RCLs have been handled by Blue Triangle. One of the first to be bought by Blue Triangle was the sole closed top example, RCL 2260. It was retained and repainted in pseudo Green Line livery in August 1999.

The Chester Bus & Boat sightseeing operation, commenced in April 1995 with open top RM 625 and RM 1836, ceased in March 1997. RM 1836 went on to operate with Bryn Melyn Motors of Llangollen from March to December 1997.

The refurbishment of Routemasters commenced again in 1997, after a two and a half year gap, with two London United RMs and four Cowie

RM 1990 operated with three other companies following sale from London Buses in October 1986, these being Gash of Newark, East Yorkshire at Scarborough and Hull and, from March 1995, with Reading Mainline. It is seen operating on Line C before this route was curtailed on 10th June 2000. RM 1990 was withdrawn on the last day of Reading Mainline operation on 22nd July 2000 and has been sold for preservation.
Andrew Morgan

For the 1998 season, K D Coach Hire operated three former Black Prince RMs along the North Wales coast, but they have not operated subsequently. All three remained in full Black Prince livery and RM 2060 is seen in April 1998 at Prestatyn Pontins. Richard Godfrey

Leaside RMs, after the route 38 tender award. Additionally, three of the former Stagecoach Bluebird RMs were transferred to Stagecoach East London and refurbished during 1997. As a direct result, in December 1997, the two RMAs were withdrawn and then converted for use by Stagecoach Portugal. Further refurbishments were carried out in early 2000 by Arriva London to provide additional vehicles for route 19. In total three RMs were refurbished to release three RMLs to be transferred to this route. From March 2000, London Central commenced the refurbishing of the RM fleet for route 36. Four contractors are involved in the work as well as London Central carrying out work themselves. Hence vehicles are operating on the route partially completed and awaiting the next work to commence. Included in this work is, for the first time, the replacement of the quarter drop windows with hopper-type windows.

Routemasters fitted with offside illuminated advert panels are now very rare indeed. Two RMLs with Arriva London North retained them on refurbishment, but these are the only RMLs so fitted. Only London Central RM 1980 remains in service with this feature. Out of the 200 bodies built with this feature, only 17 survive in the British Isles and of these only one other is currently in passenger service, this being RM 2107 with International Coachlines.

In September 1997, the Kentish Bus operation of route 19 was transferred to Cowie South London and the vehicles were repainted from their distinctive maroon and cream livery back to London red in early 1998. The Cowie operations in London with Leaside and South London were brought under the new Arriva umbrella in October 1997. In June 1997, three of the leased London Sovereign RMLs passed back to London Buses and were later passed to MTL London for continued operation. MTL London was acquired by Metroline in August 1998. Hence the original forty-six RMLs that were leased to Kentish Bus and BTS Coaches are now with Arriva London South, Sovereign and Metroline.

K & D Coach Hire of Dyserth in Denbighshire operated a service in 1998 in North Wales from Towyn to Granant via Rhyl Promenade. Three former Black Prince RMs were acquired and remained in the Black Prince livery. After this time, all three RMs were stored, until one was sold for preservation in 1999 and the remaining two passed to London Bus Services in 2000.

A new Routemaster operation based in Halifax commenced in October 1997 and built up a fleet of four RMs. However, with the increase of one-person operation, Halifax Joint Committee reduced their fleet to one RM.

London Traveller commenced operations in the late 1990s with at first railway replacement services, commercial routes in Hertfordshire and, more latterly, London Transport Bus Services routes in north west London. From April 1998, privately owned RM 2198 was used on various routes until this operator ceased to operate in Hertfordshire in July 2000 and was then returned to its owner.

Stagecoach Holdings had kept a number of Routemasters in reserve with various subsidiaries during the 1990s. Stagecoach United Counties had withdrawn their fleet in September 1993 and kept them until March 1999; the six RMs were repainted in February 1994 and then recertified every spring but only RM 682 and RM 2192 saw use during this period. Similarly Stagecoach Bluebird had withdrawn their RMs at the end of December 1996 and, although sales had taken place, three were transferred back to Stagecoach East London and two had passed to their vintage fleet; the final three were sold in November 1999. Stagecoach Cumberland had withdrawn their fleet of eight RMs in December 1992, repainted them in March 1994 and kept them until November 1999; like United Counties, Cumberland had recertified them every spring. The only one to have seen use was RM 2024 including in Lancaster and Manchester in September 1999, and Newcastle in June 1996.

When East Yorkshire withdrew their Routemaster operations from Hull in August 1995, the three refurbished RMs remained in store, whereas three others were converted to open top for the Scarborough summer sea front service. However, two of the stored RMs were sold in July 1999 and the third was converted to open top, also for service in Scarborough, in 2000.

Vintage Yellow Buses took over the former Bournemouth Routemaster vehicles and although one Routemaster, RM 219, was repainted in their attractive livery, no major operations were undertaken with these vehicles and all were sold. RMA 58 was operated on the Liverpool Heritage Circular Tour in traditional Liverpool Corporation livery of green and cream in the summers of 1996 and 1997. Another operation in Scotland was that of McGills RM 89 which lasted from 1994 until 1998.

At the time of writing, some fifteen RMs remained in semi-whole condition in the scrap yard of PVS at Barnsley after the sale of some fifty RMs for scrap from London Buses at the end of 1994. The vehicles in question are not included in the listing at the rear of this publication; they have very slowly been scrapped with any salvageable parts being recovered from them. Included in this collection of vehicles is RM 14, but this former showbus was not cannibalised and has always been kept to one side; it is currently undergoing restoration. PVS at Barnsley became the final resting place for the majority of all scrap Routemasters following the signing of a contract with London Buses in 1984. One notable dealer is Brakell Omnibus Sales who has continued to source and sell RMs since the middle 1980s to the present day.

With the reintroduction of a London administration on 3rd July 2000, which has assumed control of London Bus Services Ltd and the new organisation of Transport for London (TfL). Within a matter of weeks, the Routemaster network looked more secure than it had for many years. Although TfL want to introduce more conductors, it is not known how this will be carried out on types of vehicle other than Routemasters. One of the first changes to be announced by TfL was the cancellation of the plan to convert route 7 to low floor operation after two years of the present contract. And then it became known that TfL had authorised London Bus Services to purchase additional RMs, including initially those surplus from Reading Mainline, for use as float vehicles. Yet again second-hand Routemasters, that have operated around the country, are returning to London for further operational service!

RMA 58 was repainted into traditional Liverpool Corporation livery and used in 1996 and 1997 on the Liverpool Heritage Circular Tour.
Malcolm King

London

ARRIVA LONDON

The largest fleet of Routemasters with one operator is Arriva London with thirty-six RMs, one hundred and forty-five RMLs and two RMCs. The fleet is the combination of the former London Buses Leaside Buses and South London fleets. They were privatised and sold by London Buses on 29th September 1994 and 8th December 1994 respectively when they were acquired by the then Cowie Group plc. After Cowie acquired British Bus plc on the 18th June 1996, the newly re-formed group then changed its identity the following year, in October 1997, to Arriva plc. Outside London, the fleet livery of aquamarine and cream was adopted across the country, but with the London 80 per cent red ruling for vehicles operating on routes in central London. The Routemaster fleet remained in traditional red livery with the standard relief band. The so-called 'cow-horns' livery has not been applied to the Routemaster fleet and after trials with yellow relief bands, the new livery is all red with Arriva cream cantrail and yellow stripe running along the middle of the lower side panels and around the rear. Tottenham's RML 2635 was the first to be repainted into this livery in April 1998. To complete the new livery, the Arriva corporate fleet name was applied under the lower deck windows behind the front wheels and the strap line of 'Serving London' was applied in yellow under the fleet name.

The former Kentish Bus Iveco engined RMLs, which had latterly been based at the former London Transport Battersea garage, finally came under Arriva London control in October 1997. Between January and April 1998, the fleet of twenty-two RMLs was repainted from the maroon and cream Kentish Bus livery to the standard London red livery. Many of these vehicles

Arriva London North RMLs at Clapham garage are now appearing in a new version of the route 38 livery with the '38' in white instead of yellow and above the relief band in front of the side adverts. RML 2344 is seen at Hyde Park Corner in August 2000.
Geoff Rixon

initially received yellow relief bands. These vehicles are in fact still owned by London Transport Buses and are leased to Arriva for a nominal amount. Maintenance of these vehicles is now carried out at Brixton alongside their own RMs and RMLs and hence these vehicles have become intermixed with the RMLs from Brixton. Operationally, the Arriva London fleet is still divided into Arriva London North and Arriva London South.

All of the RMLs were refurbished between 1992 and 1994 and a start has been made on the RMs; the first done were for additional requirements for routes 38 and 19 respectively after the routes were re-tendered. With the commencement of the present contract for route 159 on 29th January 1994, the allocated RMs received the red and cream livery and some minor refurbishments (i.e. internal fluorescent lighting). These vehicles were repainted back to standard red livery with the last being completed in March 1997. When the 159 was awarded to Arriva in July 2000 a new programme of RM refurbishment was agreed which includes the fitting of Scania engines. RMC 1453 was refurbished by Leaside and returned to service in May 1996. RML 2531 received non-opening upper deck windows after accident damage early in 1996. RMs 295, 385, 736 and 1330 were acquired from the London Transport Buses Reserve fleet in February 1997 and were stored pending future requirements. RM 385 was quickly transferred to Brixton and re-engined to replace accident damaged RM 18 which was subsequently scrapped. RMs 311, 1125, 1725 and 2185 were refurbished in late-1996 and early-1997, these were followed by RM 295, 736 and 1330 during early 2000. Former London Coaches convertible open top RM 313 was acquired in late 1999 with the intention of refurbishing it and returning it to regular service; however the requirement for an extra vehicle has now passed and it remains stored with an uncertain future. With these additional vehicles, there is now a mix of RMs and RMLs at Clapton and Brixton garages which can be seen on any of the crew routes allocated. The Arriva London fleet includes some other noteworthy vehicles; they include the lowest numbered RMs – RM 5 in near original condition with AEC engine in regular use on route 38 from Clapton garage, Iveco engined RM 6 which is used alongside the regular Brixton RMs on routes 159 and 137, open top Iveco engined RMC 1464 and closed top AEC engined RMC 1453 which are part of the Leaside Travel fleet based at Edmonton, and RMLs 2544 and 2588

To release the additional vehicles required for the increased frequency for the new contract on route 19, three of the former Reserve Fleet RMs that had been in storage since 1994 were refurbished by Arriva London and entered service at Brixton where they are used on routes 137 or 159. RM 295 looks resplendent at Marble Arch in May 2000. Unusually, they were re-engined with Cummins engines rather than the Iveco units which are standard at Brixton.
Geoff Rixon

which were refurbished in the summer of 1992 and retained their offside illuminated advert panels; they are the only RMLs now so fitted.

All of the RMLs in the Arriva London North fleet are Cummins engined and those in the Arriva London South fleet are Iveco engined. The RMs have various different engines and are detailed in the main listing.

The following London Transport Buses routes are operated:

Number	Route	Operating garage	Days	pvr
19	Finsbury Park Station – Battersea Bridge	Battersea	Mon-Sat	18
38	Victoria Station – Clapton Pond	Clapton	Mon-Sat	41
73	Victoria Station – Stoke Newington Common	Tottenham	Mon-Sat	48
137	Streatham Hill – Oxford Circus	Brixton	Mon-Sat	25
159	Marble Arch – Streatham Garage	Brixton	Mon-Sat	24
			Total pvr =	156

FIRST CAPITAL

First Capital currently own one RM, but this one is not used in normal passenger service. Open-top RM 120 and closed-top RM 121 were used from 1996 by Capital Citybus. Latterly, RM 429 was also part of this fleet but was sold in April 1998. All three vehicles were used on contract and film work. Former preserved RM 1913 joined this fleet in October 1996 and was used as a training vehicle within this fleet. All three remaining Routemasters became part of First Capital in July 1998 when this company was acquired by the First Group. RM 1913 has also been used as a training vehicle within this fleet. RM 120 has also been used in passenger service on special operations and was repainted into a blue livery for use by the Conservative Party in the run up to the Mayor for London contest, returning to the standard London red livery at the close of the contract. It is normally used for private hire and contract work. RM 121 and RM 1913 left the fleet in the summer of 2000 and both passed to the London Bus Services fleet.

RM 120 ....SSL809   fleet number 920

FIRST CENTREWEST

First CentreWest operate forty-eight RMLs and one RMC. In March 1997, CentreWest was sold to the First Group; this fleet is their first subsidiary with a sizeable Routemaster operation. The fleet livery was modified to include First's f symbol in a gold-yellow colour; additionally the Gold Arrow fleet name is retained. RML 2735 is in an all red livery with CentreWest fleet names in lieu of the Gold Arrow ones so that it can be used for special occasions. First CentreWest's sole RMC, open-top RMC 1510, is used for special events, private hires and even for operation on their Routemaster routes in suitable weather conditions. Until January 1999, a second RMC was owned; it had latterly been used as a recruitment vehicle but had been out of use for a considerable period of time. Two standard RMs were acquired from the reserve fleet of London Transport Buses in 1997 but after two years of storage they were then re-sold.

All the Routemasters in the First CentreWest fleet are Cummins engined.

The following London Transport Buses routes are operated:

Number	Route	Operating garage	Days	pvr
7	Russell Square to East Acton Station	Westbourne Park	Mon-Sat	13
23	Liverpool Street Station to Westbourne Park	Westbourne Park	Mon-Sat	29
			Total pvr =	42

Above **The latest refurbishments of Routemasters by London Central include the revised livery with intermediate points shown above the lower deck windows on a distinctive blue band, new style fleet name, replacement windows and flush fitting rear registration plate, as seen on RM 1621.**
Glyn Matthews

LONDON CENTRAL/LONDON GENERAL

London Central operate thirty-eight RMs and fifty-eight RMLs whilst London General operate one RM and sixty-eight RMLs. London Central was acquired by the Go-Ahead Group plc upon privatisation in October 1994 and London General subsequently acquired in May 1996. Both companies are now managed from the same central offices at Mitcham. Generally the Routemaster operations in these companies have remained unchanged since 1994. With the exception of route 36, all the routes are operated by refurbished RMLs. The RMs on route 36 have undergone various minor refurbishments in this time including in 1995 the fitment of fluorescent strip lighting, re-trimming and repainting internally and externally. During 1997 and 1998, new Scania engines were fitted to the surviving 38 vehicles and then starting in early 2000, a full refurbishment programme was commenced. This included new floor coverings, seat moquette, new fluorescent lighting (to replace the previous type) and various other modifications, for example the replacement of the wind-down window units with hopper units. The programme was started in March 2000 and was on-going as this book was being compiled.

RM 9 was refurbished in 1997 when it was re-panelled and re-trimmed internally, including RML refurbishment moquette, and repainted in original style livery. At this time, it had its AEC engine replaced with a new Scania unit. RM 9 is noteworthy in that it is the only Routemaster in this fleet, and one of the few Routemasters in front line everyday service, that has retained its indicator ears. After the Scania re-engining programme was

Right **From June 2000, London Central started fitting these hopper window units on their refurbished RMs to replace the original wind-down type.**
Andrew Morgan

Below **The interiors are re-trimmed with RML-style seat moquette and new fluorescent tubes, while retaining the burgundy paintwork and rexine. This vehicle retains its original wind-down windows.**
Glyn Matthews

completed, all surplus RMs were sold. Vehicles operating routes 12 and 36 have carried dedicated route liveries since 1995, incorporating a vertical yellow band behind the front axle. On the refurbishment of the RMs for route 36, this livery is not being applied. RMLs 2283 and 2613 were always used for special events and private hire work and did not receive this route branding. RM 71 was latterly a training vehicle in this fleet; it was withdrawn and cannibalised for spares and has officially been written off although the shell of the body remains in New Cross garage.

London General's route 11 vehicles have been repainted in the style now being adopted for the London Central route 36 RMs. Putney's RMLs working routes 14 and 22 remain in the previous style livery, as worn by RML 2364 crossing Putney Bridge in February 2000.
Geoff Rixon

The London General fleet has retained the livery introduced in 1995 of all-over red with white relief, grey 'dog' rail with the London General fleet names on both sides and front roof dome. This has been modified on some vehicles to have the via points applied either side of the front destination box and on the sides above the lower deck windows.

Several interesting vehicles are part of the London General fleet. RM 994 is the sole RM in the London General fleet and was given a mini-refurbishment in March 1992 by Northern Counties as the prototype for other standard RMs long before the more recent programmes. RML 2745 was converted to air brakes by Dennis Specialist Vehicles in February 1992 and

London General RML 2732 is in the same livery as the well known DRM 2516 with the large gold 'General' fleetnames. Although it usually works on route 11, as seen here at Victoria, it is often used for private hire and special contracts.
Colin Lloyd

A couple of London Central RMs and RMLs have remained in the traditional London red livery with no route branding. RM 9 has also been refurbished internally and is kept in immaculate condition. It is at Victoria, on its usual haunt on route 36 in February 2000.
Tony Wilson

remains unique. RML 2516 was rebuilt with the rear end from RMC 1484 in 1991 and re-numbered DRM 2516; in February 1994 it was re-registered to WLT516. At its last repaint, it gained large gold 'GENERAL' fleet names on the sides below the lower deck windows. RML 2732 also gained this livery and these two vehicles are used for special events and private hire work.

A regular operation by the company is the use of Routemasters on routes 12, 12X and 36 on the August Bank Holiday for the Notting Hill Carnival.

In the London Central fleet, all the RMLs are Cummins engined and the RMs are Scania engined. In the London General fleet, all of the RMLs (and RM 994) are Iveco engined.

The following London Transport Buses routes are operated:

Number	Route	Operating garage	Days	pvr
11	Liverpool Street Station – Fulham Broadway	Waterloo	Mon-Fri	20
12	Notting Hill Gate – Dulwich Plough	Camberwell	Mon-Sat	38
14	Putney Heath – Tottenham Court Road Station	Putney	Mon-Sat	22
22	Putney Common – Piccadilly Circus	Putney	Mon-Sat	15
36	Queens Park Station – Lewisham	New Cross	Mon-Sat	44
			Total pvr =	139

London United acquired two of the former Reserve Fleet RMs in early 1997 and had them refurbished, although they both retain many of the original features including their AEC engines. RM 2033 is seen at Hyde Park Corner on route 9 in August 1999.
Geoff Rixon

LONDON UNITED

London United operate two RMs and thirty-nine RMLs. The company was sold in July 1997 to French transport group Transdev. Transdev is part of Caisse des Depôt et Consignations and is France's third largest bus group. The two non-standard vehicles, namely RMA 55 and RMC 1469, that had passed into the fleet upon privatisation were sold in January 1997. Meanwhile two of the former London Transport Buses reserve fleet were acquired in January 1997 and refurbished. Both retain their AEC engines but received refurbishment including new floor coverings, seat moquette, red tops to the seat frames/poles, Wareite along the interior side walls and full external repaint. Unusually, interior exposed bulbs were retained. They entered service in April 1997.

The London United Routemaster fleet has now been repainted in the post-privatisation livery of all over red with grey relief band, wheels, 'dog' rail, yellow fleet numbers, legal lettering and additional fleet numbers added beneath the nearside head lamp and rear tail light. The exception to this is the first RML, which is numbered ER 880, and retains its special Tramways style livery.

Early in 2000, London United re-registered two of their low numbered RMLs to anonymous non-matching HSLXXX registrations.

All of the RMLs in the London United fleet are Cummins engined; both of the RMs remain AEC engined.

The following London Transport Buses routes are operated:

Number	Route	Operating garage	Days	pvr
9	Hammersmith Bus Station – Aldwych	Shepherds Bush	Mon-Sat	17
94	Acton Green – Trafalgar Square	Shepherds Bush	Mon-Sat	22
			Total pvr =	39

London United sold off some of their valuable registrations early in 2000, including the registrations from two RMLs. RML 881 shows off its new registration, the London United application of a rear fleet number, including its unofficial re-designation from RML 881 to ER 881, and later style of rear light fitted on refurbishment.
Colin Lloyd

METROLINE

Metroline operate eight RMs, seventy-one RMLs (including three leased RMLs) and one RMC. The company was latterly the only management owned company after the privatisation of the London Buses companies in 1994 although the flotation of the company took place on 29th July 1997. Singapore based Delgro acquired Metroline in February 2000. To date there have been no notable changes to the company. Prior to this, in August 1998, London Northern was acquired from MTL Holdings Ltd. Since 1995 a new livery has been applied to the Routemaster fleet of all-over red, white relief band and blue radiator grille and skirt. Metroline fleet names were applied in the new style with the addition of the legend 'To and from the West End'. With the London Northern fleet came seven RMs and, with the new contract for route 10, it was decided to exchange three RMLs from Willesden garage to Holloway garage for three RMs. The RMs remain unrefurbished and retain AEC engines; it was only during 2000 that these vehicles started to be repainted into Metroline fleet livery. In late 1997/early 1998, the three former Sovereign RMLs that had been declared surplus were acquired, repainted red and entered service from Holloway garage. It is believed that all three remain owned by London Regional Transport and are on lease to Metroline. A few other Routemasters have been retained within the original Metroline fleet: open top RM 644 and closed top RMC 1513 are both used by the Contract Services fleet based at Willesden and retain original style livery; RM 70 had been used as a promotional vehicle but was sold in June 2000 after remaining out of use for a long while. Two RMs were acquired by London Northern from the London Transport reserve fleet in 1997, but these were cannibalised for spares and re-sold. From the London Northern fleet, RML 903 was never refurbished in the 1992-1994 programme and retains its original condition complete with AEC engine and various showbus features. It gained an all over red repaint in spring 2000 to improve its appearance.

Metroline operates seven RMs from Holloway and Willesden garages. During 2000 they were being repainted into full Metroline livery as can be seen by RM 1971 in mint condition at Oxford Circus in August of that year.

ROUTEMASTER HANDBOOK

Above **Metroline RML 903 is the former Finchley garage showbus and was repainted allover red in April 2000 to improve its appearance. However, it did not regain a relief band, fleet name or even a Metroline blue skirt. It is seen in New Oxford Street in June 2000.** Richard Godfrey

Right **RML 2274 is one of two of Metroline's RMLs to have been fitted with an offside brake cooling grille; the other being RML 2651. RML 2274 is seen with former London Northern RM 1799 in the yard of Willesden garage.** Andrew Morgan

All the RMLs in the Metroline fleet (except RML 903 as noted above) are Cummins engined and the RMs remain AEC engined. RML 2471 was fitted with a Cummins 5.9litre B-series Euro 2 engine in August 2000; however it was also fitted with a Allison MT643 gearbox – this is notable as the first time that a London Routemaster has had a different type of gearbox fitted in lieu of the original Wilson gearbox.

The following London Transport Buses routes are operated:

Number	Route	Operating garage	Days	pvr
6	Aldwych – Kensal Rise Station	Willesden	Mon-Sat	22
10	Hammersmith Bus Station – Archway Station	Holloway	Mon-Sat	23
98	Willesden – Holborn Red Lion Square	Willesden	Mon-Sat	21
			Total pvr =	66

STAGECOACH EAST LONDON

Just entering Oxford Street from Marble Arch in July 1998 is RM 980, which spent a period outside London with United Counties, East Midland and Stagecoach Bluebird. Returning to London in 1997, RM 980 was refurbished for operation on route 15.
Colin Lloyd

Stagecoach East London currently operate five RMs, fifty-four RMLs and three RMCs. East London was sold to Stagecoach Holdings in September 1994 and a new livery of all-over red with cream relief band and gold Stagecoach fleet names was quickly adopted for their Routemaster fleet. Three RMCs have been retained in the fleet; RMC 1456 retains red and gold route X15 livery, RM 1485 retains red and cream livery – a red version of the Green Line livery – and RMC 1461 was refurbished in the summer of 1994 in full Green Line livery. RM 613 and RM 1527 have always been used as spare vehicles at Upton Park and these two are still in original condition. Additionally, three former Stagecoach Scotland RMs, 980, 1289 and 1599, were acquired in January 1997 and refurbished during 1997. As part of the work, the rear blind boxes had to be reinstated.

The final RML, 2760, is also included within this fleet and was not included as part of the 1992–1994 London Buses RML refurbishment programme. Hence it remains to the original specification with AEC engine and internal colour scheme. It was repainted in October 1999, and regained its original livery complete with a grey relief band.

Until recently, all RMLs in the Stagecoach East London fleet were Cummins engined at Upton Park and Iveco engined at Bow but after trials in 1998, fifty-six new Scania engines were fitted to all Routemasters in this fleet except RM 613, RM 1527, the three RMCs and RML 2760, with the programme being completed in August 2000.

The two RMAs that were included in this fleet at the time of privatisation were withdrawn in December 1997. This coincided with the final introduction into service of the last of the three former Stagecoach Scotland RMs. The RMAs were then converted to open top and had their doorways moved from the left hand side to the right hand side prior to export to Portugal in April 1998 for use in the Stagecoach fleet in that country.

Above **The standard Stagecoach East London RMLs have now all been re-engined again with their Cummins or Iveco units being replaced by new Scania units. RML 2402 from Bow garage was caught in June 2000 operating route 8 through the City of London.** Richard Godfrey

Right **RMC 1485 sports a red and cream livery in Green Line style, but with Stagecoach East London fleetnames. Seen here at Aldwych in June 2000 on route 15 where it can usually be found.** Richard Godfrey

The operation of route 8 has, since late 1998, used several RMLs on Sundays because of insufficient rear-engined vehicles, making it the only standard local bus service in the UK to use Routemasters on this day at the time we prepared this book. It was expected, however, that during 2001 some further Sunday RML operation in London would begin.

The following London Transport Buses routes are operated:

Number	Route	Operating garage	Days	pvr
8	Victoria Station – Bow Church	Bow garage	Mon-Sat*	25
15	Paddington Station – East Ham	Upton Park	Mon-Sat	24
			Total pvr =	49

*See text above

Since 4th December 1993, route 13 has been operated by poppy red liveried RMLs. The tender was awarded to BTS Coaches with twenty-two refurbished RMLs prepared for the operation and leased from London Transport Buses.

BTS Coaches were taken over by Blazefield Holdings on 5th August 1994. Before the acquisition by Blazefield, a few RMs were acquired; only RM 104 was operated but this was withdrawn in October 1996 and sold to Reading Mainline in December 1996. From early June 1996, BTS Coaches was re-named London Sovereign and the fleet name of Sovereign started to be applied to the vehicles in lieu of BTS during the summer of 1996.

Until 6th July 1996, the Sunday service on the route was crew operated with the RMLs, then Olympians took over, and from 31st May 1997 the frequency of the operation was reduced and the evening operation and Sunday operation transferred to MTL London (now Metroline) with one-person operated vehicles. As fewer RMLs were now required, RMLs 2443, 2633 and 2659 were withdrawn. They were subsequently delicensed and transferred to the UniversityBus premises at Hatfield for storage. These vehicles were later repainted red and transferred to MTL London for operation at Holloway garage.

At the end of April 1999, Sovereign re-allocated its Borehamwood operation, including the nineteen leased RMLs, to part of the former London Transport garage at Edgware. Ironically, Edgware garage was one of the few London Transport garages to have never operated Routemasters.

Early in the year 2000, route 13 was re-offered for tender. However, it became common knowledge that Sovereign were not interested in a further contract term with this route, preferring to concentrate their resources on the Harrow and Edgware network of routes. The contract was extended to August 2001 and re-offered for tender. This time Sovereign did submit a bid and in December 2000 were re-awarded the contract for the operation of the route with Routemasters to be used daytime Mondays to Saturdays. The RMLs are to be exchanged for some of the London Bus Services RMs which by then will have been refurbished and re-engined with the Cummins B-series Euro 2 engine complete with the Allison MT643 gearbox.

Stored in Ash Grove garage at the beginning of 2001 were a number of RMs purchased by London Bus Services Ltd, the bulk intended for route 13 later in the year. Andrew Morgan

The following London Transport Buses route is operated:

Number	Route	Operating garage	Days	pvr
13	Golders Green Station – Aldwych	Edgware	Mon-Sat	18
			Total pvr =	18

LONDON BUS SERVICES LTD

In December 2000 London Bus Services Ltd (LBSL) owned thirty-three RMs and forty-six RMLs.

The refurbished RMLs used by Arriva London South on route 19, London Sovereign on route 13 and three RMLs used by Metroline on route 10, are owned by London Bus Services Ltd (LBSL) and are leased to the operating companies.

With the election of the Mayor for London from 3rd July 2000, a distinct policy on the Routemaster quickly became apparent. With the re-award of route 159, Transport for London announced that the Routemaster is to be kept on the road. To provide a float of vehicles for the London routes, more RMs have been acquired. The intended use of these is initially so that there are enough vehicles to allow the refurbishment of other Routemasters and secondly to bolster the fleet.

The first vehicles to be acquired were nine of the final Reading Mainline fleet. Other surplus RMs are also being sourced, mainly from stock from dealers. It is planned to re-engine this fleet with the Cummins 5.9 litre B-series Euro 2 engine with the Allison MT643 gearbox (as first fitted to Metroline RML 2471); the first RM was dispatched to Cummins at Wellingborough in January 2001. Additionally these RMs will be refurbished before their use in London from the summer of 2001, principally on Sovereign route 13 to release RMLs for use elsewhere.

RM 23 .... JFO256	RM 875 .... OSV940	RM 1650 ...... 650DYE
RM 45 .... AST415A	RM 931 .... MFF580	RM 1735 ...... 735DYE
RM 121 .... SSL806	RM 1005 ...... ALC290A	RM 1913 ...... ALD913B
RM 180 .... XVS830	RM 1018 ...... PVS828	RM 1933 ...... ALD933B
RM 191 .... AST416A	RM 1204 ...... 204CLT	RM 1941 ...... ALD941B
RM 324 .... WLT324	RM 1218 ...... 218CLT	RM 2060 ...... ALM60B
RM 329 .... MFF578	RM 1245 ...... LDS210A	RM 2071 ...... ALM71B
RM 441 .... LDS341A	RM 1280 ...... 280CLT	RM 2089 ...... ALM89B
RM 659 .... KFF239	RM 1312 ...... MFF509	RM 2122 ...... CUV122C
RM 838 .... XYJ440	RM 1568 ...... BNK324A	
RM 848 .... WLT848	RM 1627 ...... 627DYE	
RM 871 .... WLT871	RM 1640 ...... 640DYE	

RML 2265 .... CUV265C	RML 2512 .... JJD512D	RML 2591 .... JJD591D
RML 2266 .... CUV266C	RML 2514 .... JJD514D	RML 2598 .... JJD598D
RML 2301 .... CUV301C	RML 2523 .... JJD523D	RML 2619 .... NML619E
RML 2322 .... CUV322C	RML 2524 .... JJD524D	RML 2627 .... NML627E
RML 2341 .... CUV341C	RML 2527 .... JJD527D	RML 2633 .... NML633E
RML 2343 .... CUV343C	RML 2531 .... JJD531D	RML 2659 .... SMK659F
RML 2347 .... CUV347C	RML 2533 .... JJD533D	RML 2663 .... SMK663F
RML 2382 .... JJD382D	RML 2536 .... JJD536D	RML 2668 .... SMK668F
RML 2383 .... JJD383D	RML 2538 .... JJD538D	RML 2674 .... SMK674F
RML 2387 .... JJD387D	RML 2548 .... JJD548D	RML 2686 .... SMK686F
RML 2404 .... JJD404D	RML 2563 .... JJD563D	RML 2694 .... SMK694F
RML 2410 .... JJD410D	RML 2569 .... JJD569D	RML 2715 .... SMK715F
RML 2443 .... JJD443D	RML 2574 .... JJD574D	RML 2719 .... SMK719F
RML 2452 .... JJD452D	RML 2577 .... JJD577D	RML 2759 .... SMK759F
RML 2487 .... JJD487D	RML 2582 .... JJD582D	
RML 2505 .... JJD505D	RML 2586 .... JJD586D	

CURRENT UK PSV USERS

London sightseeing operations

ARRIVA TOLST

Arriva The Original London Sightseeing Tour, as it is now known, was previously well known as the sightseeing company London Coaches. The fleet consists of ten ERMs, six RMs and two convertible open top RCLs, although three of the RCLs have been withdrawn for some time and may be sold. London Coaches was the first of the London Buses operating subsidiaries to be privatised on 18th May 1992 when it was sold to its management. The sightseeing operation of London Coaches was sold on 4th December 1997 to Arriva; the trading name London Coaches was retained by North Kent Express based at Northfleet. Initially, the only obvious sign of any change was the re-registering of four ERMs with JSJ74x registrations. These vehicles now carry revised ERM numbers to match their new registrations. The Routemaster fleet has reduced as these and other vehicles in the fleet have been replaced by newly converted open top former Arriva London Metrobuses.

The standard livery was applied from late 1998, but was not seen on Routemasters in service until Easter 1999 and is the Arriva inspired red and cream. Several vehicles are painted in various advertising liveries; they include RM 752 (British Tourist Authority) and RM 1919 (Harrods). RM 545, RM 753, RCL 2220 and RCL 2248 currently carry all over red livery for use as dedicated private hire vehicles.

Since May 1992, the Routemaster fleet has gradually been reduced, with the last RMAs leaving in October 1994, sales of the RCLs commencing in March 1997 and the last of the convertible open top RMs departing in

ERM 46 (formerly ERM 90) and her sisters entered service at Easter 1999 in the new Arriva The Original London Sightseeing Tour livery. Four of the ten ERMs were re-registered in late 1997, having lost their VLT registrations at the time of the sale of the London Coaches sightseeing operations to Arriva. When repainted in their present livery they were re-numbered to match their new registrations.
Tony Wilson

Two RMs and two RLCs are kept in red livery rather than the Arriva inspired red and off white colour scheme. RCL 2220 is one such example and, unusually, retained the London Coaches fleetname when photographed at Victoria in April 2000.
Tony Wilson

December 1999. The majority of vehicles leaving the fleet over the last six years have found continued use in passenger service with their new owners. The unique ERM fleet has remained intact. One wheelchair accessible vehicle remains in the fleet, namely RM 307; the other, RM 450, passed to London Coaches at Northfleet. RM 1864 is the last Leyland engined Routemaster owned by a central London company. The sole closed-top RM is the DAF engined RM 545; this vehicle was fitted with this engine in April 1988.

Currently, apart from RM 545 and RM 1864, all Routemasters in this fleet retain AEC engines although it has been rumoured for some time that another type of engine may be fitted instead.

In October 1997 RM 752 was repainted in an allover livery promoting the British Tourist Authority, a livery which it still carries.
Colin Lloyd

In July, open-top RM 1919 was repainted into full Harrods livery when the sightseeing subsidiary of Arriva took over the operation of the Harrods sightseeing service.
Geoff Rixon

ERM 46 [1]	..... JSJ746	ERM 143	...... VLT143	ERM 242	...... VLT242
ERM 47 [2]	..... JSJ747	ERM 163	...... VLT163	ERM 281	...... VLT281
ERM 48 [3]	..... JSJ748	ERM 235	...... VLT235		
ERM 49 [4]	..... JSJ749	ERM 237	...... VLT237		

ERMs originally numbered: [1] – ERM 90; [2] – ERM 84; [3] – ERM 80; [4] – ERM 94.

RCL 2220	...... CUV220C	RCL 2248	...... CUV248C		
RM 307	.... WLT307	RM 752	.... WLT752	RM 1864	..... 864DYE
RM 545	.... WLT545	RM 753	.... WLT753	RM 1919	..... ALD919B

For this operation the interior has been totally re-trimmed, with seats turned around and covered in leather and wooden tables fitted.
Geoff Rixon

BIG BUS

Big Bus currently operate one RM and three RMF vehicles on its London sightseeing operation. The Big Bus Company commenced the operation of Routemasters with former Blue Triangle open top FPT588C from April 1992 onwards. It had been acquired after conversion to open top and was repainted in their maroon and cream livery after having its front blind box removed and panelled over. Similar former Northern General RMF FPT592C was acquired in February 1995 and, after repaint in September, entered service in the November of the same year. Unlike FPT588C, the front blind box of this previously preserved vehicle remains intact and in use. Former promotional vehicle, and Cadbury's 'Stroller' liveried RM 272 was acquired in October 1995 and entered service in February 1996 after having its blind boxes removed and a full repaint into the fleet livery. RM 272 is numbered as RM 236 to match its registration number. Both RM 272 and FPT592C were retrimmed in the original style RM moquette. Additionally, the interior of RM 272 was repainted brown with cream ceilings. In January 1996, two further Routemasters were acquired. The first to see use was FPT603C which after repaint entered service in December 1996 and was notable as the first Routemaster in their fleet with a maroon roof. RM 10 was also acquired but this remained in storage until sold in February 2000.

FPT603C (originally with Northern General) had operated with Timothy Ashton Hospitality Buses for seven years and was then restored when preserved in 1990, but unusually with London style blind box and wind down windows. It has operated with Big Bus since 1996.

Andrew Morgan

RM 272 .... LDS236A

RMF 588 ...... FPT588C
RMF 592 ...... FPT592C
RMF 603 ...... FPT603C

Outside London

BATH BUS COMPANY

Since 1997 RM 1783 has operated with the Bath Bus Company. This is the third company that has operated this particular vehicle in open top form.
Andrew Morgan

Former London Coaches open top RM 1783 was acquired in April 1997. It entered service at the end of May 1997 alongside Bristol VRs used in Bath. This Routemaster was originally converted to open top for the Liverpool Garden Festival in 1986.

RM 1783 ...... 783DYE

THE BIG RED BUS

Convertible open top RCL is branded for 'The Purbeck Tour' and operates in open top mode from Swanage during the summer months. These vehicles are also used for school contracts including schoolday service C2 (Gillingham to Marnhull).

RMA 62 .... NMY662E   RMA 65 .... NMY665E   RCL 2253 ...... CUV253C

Formerly with London Coaches, Redbus RMA 65 retains its red and off-white livery when leaving Gillingham School in Dorset in May 2000.
Derek Persson

BIRKENHEAD TRAMWAY MUSEUM

Iveco engined RM 1101 was acquired from London Buses by A1A Travel in September 1994. Since 1995, it has been used on school contracts to the Birkenhead Tram Museum at Pacific Road where it is garaged. It was acquired by Friends of Wirral Transport Museum in June 1997 and has continued in use in connection in the museum as well as on route 15 to and from New Brighton. It was re-registered from KGH969A to KFF367 in October 1995. It has remained in London red livery with cream relief band and London Transport fleet names and was last repainted in February 1997.

RM 1101 ...... KFF367

Iveco engined RM 1101 was formerly with A1A Travel and is now owned by Wirral Transport Museum who regularly use it in connection with Birkenhead Tramway Museum. This picture was taken in October 1998 at the Wirral Bus and Tram Show.
Reg Wilson

RM 560 was operated by Magicbus and then Stagecoach Bluebird from May 1985 to December 1996 when it was withdrawn from operation in Perth. In July 1997 it was repainted into A1 Service livery and the following month was seen at Irvine Cross when it was briefly operated by Stagecoach Western. *Billy Nicol*

BLUEBIRD

Stagecoach Bluebird own two RMs and one RMA; these are the remnants of the Perth Routemaster operation that was withdrawn on 27th December 1996. All three form part of the Stagecoach preserved fleet and are stored at the Scottish Vintage Bus Museum at Lathalmond. RM 1607 and RMA 50 remain in full Stagecoach livery. RM560 was repainted into A1 livery in August 1997. It was used in 1997 on route 11 (Kilmarnock to Ardrossan) alongside Stagecoach A1 Service liveried N and P prefix registered Volvo Olympians. It was rumoured that another RM was to be repainted into the green livery of AA Buses of Ayr but this was never carried out and the remaining three RMs were sold at the end of 1999.

After nearly three years of ownership, Blue Triangle repainted RCL 2260 in pseudo Green Line livery, using their own transfers instead of Green Line fleet names. It is here operating a free service in early November 1999. *Andrew Morgan*

RM 560 .... EDS50A   RM 1607 ...... LDS201A   RMA 50 .... NMY634E

BLUE TRIANGLE

Blue Triangle of Rainham was owned and managed from the start by a group of enthusiasts. As the name suggests, most of their original vehicles were built by AEC. At various times, they have operated RM, RMA, RMC, open top RMF and RCL types, as well as acting as dealers by selling on several RMs and most of the former London Coaches RMAs. Their open top RMF was sold in March 1992, and RMA 49 and RCL 2239 passed to Imperial Buses (which was initially known as Croftpeak) in early 1999.

As a replacement for RCL 2239, RCL 2260 was restored from the sales stock and repainted in August 1999 into Green Line livery but with gold Blue Triangle fleet names in the traditional positions. It has been noted in use at various times on routes 204 (Loughton – Debden) and 265 (Romford – Bulphan).

In January 1995, Blue Triangle acquired RML 900 from Clydeside 2000, but to date have not operated this vehicle and it is undergoing restoration prior to possible use by this operator. Various other vehicles are owned, including Routemasters of various types, but are not part of the operational fleet. Some vehicles are only dealer stock and are usually sold on in due course, but may occasionally enter the operational fleet. Vehicles that come into this category include RM 85, RM 111, RM 298 and RM 1936.

The Routemasters in the Blue Triangle operational fleet are:

RCL 2260 ..... CUV260C   RML 900 ...... WLT900

CONFIDENCE BUS & COACH

Confidence Bus & Coach Hire of Oadby still operate Leyland engined RM 655 in their fleet. It came to them direct from London Buses in August 1985 and was repainted in their black and grey livery complete with red lining. A second

Leyland engined RM 655 has been owned by Leicester based Confidence since August 1985. It is seen leaving Bourne operating in passenger service for the Delaine running day in 1996.
Andrew Morgan

Leyland engine Routemaster, RM 621, was acquired in June 1986, but was sold in October 1990 after receiving severe accident damage. The remaining vehicle continues to be used on school contracts and services connected with the Leicester University.

RM 655 .... WLT655   fleet number 15

EAST YORKSHIRE

Former Kelvin Scottish RM 1010 has operated with East Yorkshire since July 1994, but was converted to open-top in April 1996 for operation with Scarborough & District on its sea front service.
Dave Brown

East Yorkshire currently own five RMs, of which four have been converted to open top. Originally seven Routemasters were acquired direct from London Buses in April 1988 for operation on routes 56 and 56A in Hull from 3rd May 1988. The fleet was repainted in the traditional and very attractive livery of indigo, primrose and white. The fleet continued to increase in size with the acquisition of a total of 19 vehicles for service and a further five for spares. RM 727 was the first of three RMs to be refurbished internally early in 1993 by SYT at Rotherham. From 28th February 1995, the crew operation was revised. Some nine RMs were withdrawn to leave only the routes 56/56A along the Holderness Road. This further rationalisation of the routes between East Yorkshire and Stagecoach-owned Kingston-upon-Hull (KHCT) took place as the Routemasters had been too successful on the jointly operated routes 3 and 4 (i.e. the East Yorkshire crew buses were operating the route more quickly than the opo vehicles run by KHCT).

Former Clydeside Scottish RM 727 was refurbished in December 1992 and was held back as a reserve vehicle from August 1995 until converted to open-top in 1999. It entered service at Scarborough for the 2000 summer season. Dave Brown

Routemaster operation finally ceased on Saturday 13th August 1995 after some seven years of operation. This was ahead of the forthcoming Holderness Road Bus Priority Scheme and the proposed introduction of Smart cards with the eventual hope of matching the running times achieved by the RMs. RM 188 was retained in the East Yorkshire traditional livery within the vintage vehicle fleet and sees occasional use. Initially the three refurbished RMs were retained in store, but in 1999 RM 732 and 798 were sold and later exported. RMs 1010, 2065 and 2210 were converted to open top in 1996 by East Yorkshire and joined the existing operations at Scarborough displacing younger Bristol VRs. RM 727 was also converted to open top in early 1999, but did not enter service until the 2000 season. Several members of this fleet of Routemasters carry all over advertisement liveries which are usually varied for each season. For the 1998 season, the Scarborough & District livery, whether with an all over advert or not, had the addition of large bows over the front blind boxes.

RM 188	VLT188		fleet number 808
RM 727	LDS239A	R OT	fleet number 817
RM 1010	EDS221A	OT	fleet number 819
RM 2065	ALM65B	OT	fleet number 812
RM 2210	CUV210C	OT	fleet number 816

R – refurbished   OT – open top

Four RMs were operated by Halifax Joint Committee until October 2000, all painted in different liveries. This one is RM 1214 which is the only one retained. It was photographed at Halifax Bus Station in April 1999. Tony Wilson

HALIFAX JOINT COMMITTEE

Halifax Joint Committee commenced Routemaster operation on 13th October 1997 with former London Buses reserve fleet RMs 324 and 1204. Both had been repainted into full traditional Halifax livery albeit each in a different style. A network of routes has been built up around the Halifax, Hebden Bridge and Sowerby Bridge areas. A third Routemaster, namely RM 1214, was acquired in November 1997 and was repainted in another variation of the livery. A fourth RM, RM 659, was acquired in January 1999 and was operated in as acquired London red livery. At the time of writing, nine Metrobuses and five Leyland Nationals have been acquired to operate the one person operated routes on the Halifax Joint Committee network and, until 6th October 2000, four Routemasters saw regular use on routes 17, 22, 28, 29A, 34, 36 and 36A. However, the Routemaster operations were reduced after this date with the sale of three of the RMs to London Bus Services. Over the last five years, as engines have been changed, the Routemasters have received the larger 11.3 litre AV690 engine; with these the Routemasters' performance was improved on the hills around Halifax. In addition, the AEC Regent BCP671 is also operated from time to time.

RM 1214 ...... 214CLT

In June 1999 RMA 49 was painted into this livery for Croftpeak Services by Blue Triangle, who had used it since 1992 including for sightseeing operations. Croftpeak subsequently amalgamated with Imperial Buses who have a green based livery, although this particular vehicle has yet to receive it.
Andrew Morgan

IMPERIAL BUSES

Former Blue Triangle RMA 49 and RCL 2239 passed to Croftpeak in early 1999. They have been loaned to various operators and continue in use on rail replacement services. RCL 2239 remains in the Blue Triangle red and cream livery although with fleet names removed. RMA 49 had latterly been numbered RMS 49 but when repainted in June 1999 it gained a two tone red and cream livery which has been likened to the old Barton livery. Upon repaint, it was given Croftpeak fleet names, but this company name has since been dropped and these vehicles are operated by Imperial Buses of Rainham in Essex.

RCL2239 ...... CUV239C   RMA49 .... NMY632E

INTERNATIONAL COACHLINES

International Coachlines currently operate four RMs, two RMAs and one RMF. International Coachlines was previously known as Time Travel until the trading name was changed during 1996. Their first Routemaster was

RMA 52 which was acquired from North Mymms Coaches in August 1992. Former Northern General RCN701 was acquired in November 1992 and restored to psv operation in November 1994. Previously it had been a non-psv with Timothy Ashton Hospitality Buses of Epsom. RCN701 was numbered RMF 2771 when acquired in 1980 by London Transport. Iveco engined RM 1083 was acquired from London Buses via PVS at Barnsley (albeit collected directly from the former) in October 1994 and had platform doors fitted before entering service in the summer of 1995. Additionally, RMA 57 (BEA 54) has been used by this operator since the spring of 1995. The other three RMs were all acquired from preservationists and like RM 1083 have had rear platform doors fitted in the same style as an RMC. The RMF and RM 2107 are Leyland engined, whilst the RMAs and RMs 259 and 471 are AEC engined.

In June 1998, a Friday-only route 709 was introduced (Caterham via Thornton Heath and Elephant & Castle to Chase Farm Hospital in Enfield). RMA 57 was the usual vehicle on this route and looked most odd with its blinds stuck directly to the bodywork. After 15th December, route 709 was re-routed at its northern destination to Waltham Cross and increased operation to Tuesdays and Fridays. This route even operated on Christmas

RMA 57 was the regular vehicle used on International Coachlines long route 709. This vehicle had blind boxes fitted to the front and under the canopy, seen here being adjusted, but still had blinds stuck directly onto the bodywork on the offside staircase panel, when caught at Caterham Station in October 1998.
John G.S. Smith

ROUTEMASTER HANDBOOK

Above **Typical of the standard Routemasters operated by International Coachlines is RM 259, having been rebuilt with RMC style platform doors. It was photographed in Parliament Square in August 2000.**
Geoff Rixon

Right **RM 2107 has had modern glider doors fitted instead of the more usual 4-leaf doors as originally fitted to RMCs and RCLs.**
Andrew Morgan

Day 1998 (using their RMF) and New Years Day 1999. On Christmas Day 1999, RMA 52 operated on route 709. This route has now been withdrawn except on Christmas Day, but the Routemasters in this fleet continue in regular use on private hire and contract work.

From 12th May to 14th July 1998, privately owned RM 548 was loaned to this operator, but it was not acquired.

RM 259	...... VLT259	RMA 52	..... NMY637E
RM 471	...... KVS601	RMA 57	..... NMY654E
RM 1083	...... XVS850	RMF 2771	..... RCN701
RM 2107	...... CUV107C		

LIVERPOOL MOTOR SERVICES

RM 1449 has seen occasional use with various Liverpool operators since it was sold from Kelvin Central Buses in 1993. Most recently, it has seen use from October 1998 with Liverpool Motor Services of Aintree. Also owned by this operator is RMA 58 (NMY655E) which was last used in service in Liverpool Corporation livery of green and cream in 1996 and 1997 when it operated the Liverpool Heritage Circular Tour service; it has not however been seen in operation since.

RM 1449 ...... 449CLT

MAC TOURS

Two former preserved Routemasters were acquired by Edinburgh sightseeing operator Mac Tours in late 1999. Former Kelvin RM 371 has been converted to open top, although by August 2000 had not been finished. It is planned to convert RM 2203 to convertible open top but at the time of writing, work had not commenced on this vehicle. RMA 9 was acquired in November 2000. It is to be re-seated after use as a publicity vehicle by its previous owner and may be converted to open-top. The standard livery for this operator is red and cream, and it is expected that in due course the Routemasters will be repainted into this livery.

In the summer of 2000 McKindless repainted this Leyland engined RM 1966 from its former Reading Mainline livery to this equally attractive traditional scheme which is similar in application to that of Central SMT.
Malcolm King

RM 371 .... WLT371   RM 2203 ...... CUV203C
RMA 9 .... NMY646E

McKINDLESS

Former Reading Mainline RM 1966 was acquired by McKindless of Wishaw in October 1999. This RM was repainted into Central SMT Scottish red and cream livery complete with advertisements for the various McKindless companies including the flower shop and body shop.

RM 1966 ...... ALB966B   fleet number 1950

RMC 1490 was repainted in early 2000 ready for use by Metrobus. By the autumn of 2000, necessary rectification work had not been completed. Chris Suggit

METROBUS

Privately owned RMC 1490 was repainted in full Metrobus blue livery with a yellow relief band in March 2000. It was intended to use this Routemaster on Sunday route 473 (East Grinstead to Kingscote Station) for the Bluebell Railway. At the time of writing, it had not entered passenger service.

RMC 1490 .... 490CLT

NORTH KENT EXPRESS

North Kent Express is the former London Coaches Kent commuter coach operations that operate daily from various Kent towns to central London. One Routemaster was retained, and did not pass to Arriva in December 1997, namely RM 450. This RM was one of two that had been fitted with a wheel-chair lift in September 1988 but this feature had latterly been removed as this vehicle had been used as an exhibition vehicle. In 1997 it had been used by Medway FM radio station. During the summer of 1998, open top RM 450 was used on a hop-on hop-off sightseeing tour of the Medway towns including Chatham, Rochester and Gillingham.

RM 450 .... WLT450

Nostalgiabus currently own six RMs. The company commenced operations in spring 1992 with private hire and tour work using mainly vintage type vehicles. Additionally, vehicles are frequently seen on rail replacement services. Vehicles are operated from a base in Mitcham. At times of vehicle shortages, RMC 1462 was often hired out to other operators, including Green Rover in 1992 and Timebus in 1995–6, coincidentally for operation in the same town, Watford.

Between 1st May and 25th September 1994, Nostalgiabus operated route 693 from Morden Hall Garden Centre to Merton Abbey Mills. RMC 1462 was loaned to London & Country in June and July 1995 to cover for the absent RM 1183 on Sunday route 410. Conversely, RM 121 was frequently hired from LBPG at Cobham to assist with various private hire and school contracts.

Six of the former Timebus/Watford & District RMs, including RM 357 in the Maidstone & District inspired Watford & District livery were acquired in April 1997. Initially they saw occasional use on school routes 676 and 678, but from 13th December 1997, new route 306 (Kingston, Tolworth, Ewell to Epsom) was introduced. This was the first new Routemaster operated route in the London area since March 1992, although this route did also have one person vehicles allocated as well. RM 1183 suffered accident damage in December 1997, only to be repaired and then written off after being destroyed by fire less than four weeks later. Former London Northern RM 1081 was acquired as a source of spare parts to repair RM 1183 and then

RM 1394 had previously operated with Timebus and briefly with Watford & District before being acquired by Nostalgiabus in April 1997. It is seen fresh from repaint when operating on route 306 in October 1999.
Geoff Rixon

RM 1571 was accidentally de-roofed in September 1999 and was subsequently rebuilt to permanent open top in May 2000. Unusually, apart from the first two open top conversions in the UK, RM 1403 and RM 581, all conversions have retained their rear emergency exit and have two side window bays at the front whereas Nostalgiabus RM 1571 has only one window bay. Geoff Rixon

fire damaged RM 1571. Christmas 1997 saw RMC 1462 used on Surrey County Council route 93 (Dorking to Horsham). Other routes to have seen Routemaster operation by this operator include route LT route 60 (from January to March 1999), 70D, 710, LT route 127, school route 518 and school route 808. Route 306 was withdrawn on 25th July 1998 as a result of route changes in Surrey. RMC 1462 was de-roofed in May 1998 but was repaired using the roof from RM 357 which was to be converted to open top. On 13th September 1999, route 306 was re-introduced but with limited journeys only and between Banstead and Walton-on-the-Hill via Epsom and Tadworth. RM 1571 was de-roofed in September 1999 in Southend Lane, Sydenham, while on a wedding contract. It was later converted to full open top in May 2000 by Ensign Bus.

RMC 1462 passed back to its owner in early summer 2000.

RM 357 .... YVS288	RM 1394 ...... 394CLT	RM 2156 ...... CUV156C
RM 378 .... WFO410	RM 1571 ...... 571CLT	RM 2180 ...... CUV180C

ROUTE 24

From Easter 1995, RM 24 has been operated in the Bournemouth area by Mr C. Kilby trading as Route 24. RM 24 has latterly been used on private hire work.

RM 24 .... VLT24

SHAFTESBURY & DISTRICT

Shaftesbury & District currently own one RMA although various other vehicles have been owned since 1987. Routemaster operation became a part of this company after the ashes of Verwood Transport had settled. Based in the Dorset town of Motcombe, Shaftesbury & District operated local bus services, school transport and private hire work in the Shaftesbury and Salisbury areas with RMA 37 in their fleet. This vehicle was acquired from the scrapyard of PVS at Barnsley in 1987 and consequently featured various non-standard (to an RMA type vehicle) items e.g. opening front windscreen, canopy blind box, RMC type front blind box and, at one time, non-opening front upper deck windows. RMA 37 was subsequently sold to Timebus in October 1996. A second former BEA Routemaster was acquired in March 1992 after lying dormant in the yard of Wombwell Diesels. It had been a training vehicle with London Buses and more recently owned by Clydeside/Western Scottish but rarely used. RMA 10 was acquired from Routemaster Travel in February 1996 for possible future use and was sold in September 1997. Former Confidence RM621 was rebuilt by Shaftesbury & District during the winter of 1992/1993 and made its début at the Cobham gathering on 4th April 1993 before being repainted and placed on long term loan to Routemaster Bournemouth. It was subsequently sold to Reading Mainline in October 1994. Similarly, RMC 1477 was acquired in May 1993 and was rebuilt and restored to passenger service prior to sale to Blue Triangle in August 1994.

RMA 29 was rebuilt over a number of years and was extended by one full

Shaftesbury & District RME 1 was licensed for service for one month only in July 2000. It initially appeared at the Routemaster Day at Cobham Bus Museum and then, on the 28th July, it was used on Verwood Bus route V1 and is seen here at Poole. Michael Wadham

Inset As RME 1 was rebuilt with a centre staircase, this enabled an opening to be built between the driver's cab and the lower saloon. Also visible is the ticket machine baseplate as this vehicle is intended to be one person operated. Andrew Morgan

Routemaster body bay in length (i.e. it is now the same length as an ERM). It has had a staircase from a former Clydeside Ailsa fitted in the centre and has had the front bulkhead altered so that the driver can gain access to the interior of the vehicle; this is so that the vehicle can be one-person operated. Additionally, it now has non-opening upper deck windows, single head lamps (although these were fitted by London Buses in the 1980s) and a front single piece blind box. It has been re-numbered as RME 1 (Routemaster Extended). It was first licensed at the end of June 2000 and made its public début at the Routemaster Day at Cobham Museum on 2nd July 2000.

RME 1 .... KGJ603D

SULLIVAN BUSES

Sullivan Buses was set up in 1999 and currently operates one RM. Sullivan Buses is the former Potters Bar based company previously known as Sidney Road Travel. Former preserved RM 1069 is operated alongside a fleet of former London Titans, Metrobuses and one Dennis Dart. As well as private hire and rail replacement work, two night routes are operated in the Watford area on Friday and Saturday nights.

RM 1069 ...... 69CLT

RM 1069 has been occasionally used in passenger service since 1995 but since 1999 it has been used regularly by Sullivan Bus. It is seen on the railway replacement service which was substituting for the southern end of the Victoria Line in August 2000.
Geoff Rixon

TIMEBUS

Timebus Travel have always undertaken private hire and contract work and currently operate two RMs and one RMA. However, they commenced their first commercial service in St Albans in March 1993. The livery, of red with flake grey bands around the upstairs windows and below the lower deck windows as well as in the standard central relief position, is retained today. The initial service only lasted until May 1993, but a new operation in Watford commenced in July 1994. This operation was increased and additional vehicles were acquired until November 1996 when seven Routemasters were then owned. However, in February 1997 all existing operations of Timebus were taken over by new operator Watford & District. Due to severe competition with Arriva The Shires, this new operator lasted only seventeen days. The fleet of Timebus Routemasters all passed to Watford & District but after this short operation, RM 1871 and RMA 37 returned to the Timebus fleet.

Timebus work has subsequently continued as before, but without the commercial operations. In May 1999, former London Coaches convertible open top RM 479 was acquired.

In July 2000, a one day a week sightseeing operation commenced in St Albans, for a two month operation.

Timebus vehicles are mainly used for private hire and contract work but RMA 37 is seen in June 1997 on special route 354A on the occasion of the St Albans Bus rally.
Andrew Morgan

RM 479 .... WSJ737   RM 1871 ...... ALD871B   RMA 37 .... KGJ612D

Immaculate RM 1871 is seen at Marble Arch in August 2000 being used for a wedding. RM 1871 has previously operated with Southend Transport and Southampton City Transport. Geoff Rixon

TOUREX

Tourex of Oxford acquired Iveco engined RM 1528 in April 2000 and it is reported as being prepared for future use.

RM 1528 ...... KGJ117A

YORKSHIRE BELLES

The Yorkshire Belles Yesteryear Tour commenced from 2nd May 1994 as a niche sightseeing operation in York. Initially former Southend Transport RCL 2256 was loaned from Brakell until the arrival of their own vehicle. RM 388 arrived on 21st May 1994 and like the RCL was painted in an all-over maroon livery with a gold band. However, the RM was unusually rebuilt by Kent Coachworks with an open rear staircase. RCL 2256 was returned to Brakell Omnibus Sales in July 1994. The tour of York with RM 388 was a seasonal operation but has not been operated regularly since 1998.

RM 388 .... EDS300A

RM 2129 was one of the last surplus vehicles to be sold by London Buses in 1994 and is now owned by Freight Media. It has been used in many liveries and in June 1999 was used for a free bus service to the Wimbledon Tennis tournament.
Graham Lunn

With all types of double-deck bus, a certain percentage will always find new uses as publicity vehicles or hospitality units, mobile canteens or playbuses. The Routemaster is no exception, and the popularity of this bus has produced some unusual results. RM 110 is perhaps the ultimate show vehicle since it has been customised. It is now approximately two feet lower in height and has been fitted with a bar and juke box. However, it has not been seen at shows since 1993 and is currently for sale.

Conversion to open-top for promotional use is not uncommon; RM 581 is used by a local newspaper and RM 238 is with a children's entertainer (although not in use yet) with this style of bodywork. Other promotional vehicles include RMs 245, 255, 548, 843 and RMC 1496. Of these RM 255 has appeared in a distinctive turquoise livery for Green Bohemia Ltd who are importers of Absinth liqueur. In total three vehicles are currently used as playbuses, RM 1878, RM 1790 and RCL 2218, with RM 2178 used by a children's entertainer.

RM 216 was extensively rebuilt as a project vehicle for GEC-Marconi Electronics and was fitted with many electronic items of equipment for its new role. RM 29 was reported in use as an Internet café in November 1998, but further sightings have not been recorded. RM 376 is used on several farms in Lincolnshire to transport workers. It was acquired to replace prewar RT 77. Former Magicbus RM 831 has been used by Auto Recoveries as a turnover vehicle at various shows in north west England. RM 811, a former CDS and London Coaches vehicle, was donated by London Transport to the David Shepherd Foundation on 26th July 1994 in exchange for a painting of a 1966 RML (with a pair of RTs and various contemporary vehicles) on Westminster Bridge. It is now used as a promotional vehicle for the foundation. RM 697, RM 1776 and RMC 1495 have been converted into roadside cafés although not all are regularly used. RM 1185 was until recently parked in Lower Marsh in Waterloo awaiting further use; it had been intended to convert it into a coffee bar. RM 872 has been used by the British Broadcasting Corporation since late 1999 in connection with 'beeb.com' and has been equipped with numerous television screens and computers. RM 966 is used by Nacro around Hastings and Bexhill teaching people basic IT skills. RM 1643 is used by the Renal Unit at the Queen Elizabeth Hospital at Edgbaston to raise funds for their charities and has even travelled around Europe. RM 1274 is now in a multicoloured livery as a mobile youth club and is based in the Woking area. Former Reading Mainline RM 1357 was sold in March 2000 apparently for conversion internally into the layout of a submarine. This vehicle is now in an all-over white livery with most, if not all, windows panelled over. RM 1771 was originally part of the batch of vehicles that were to be scrapped by North's of Sherburn-in-Elmet after the

RM 238 was acquired by Fuzzy Duzzy Children's Entertainer in late 1999, but has so far not been used. It was previously in a yellow livery for the Bucks Free Press, as illustrated on the front cover of the first edition of this book. Bob Martin

RM 125 has been used to promote Snickers chocolate bars although has not been owned by Freight Media throughout this period. It is seen at Woolaton Park in Nottingham in May 1997.
Andrew Morgan

first withdrawals in 1982. However, it survived, and has been put to a variety of uses including being hired to various companies to provide a bus service or for film work. Currently it is owned by a Night club in Doncaster. Similarly RM 2186 has seen use with the Tuxedo Princess Nightclub in Newcastle. Former Rotherham & District and Greater Manchester Buses RM 1807 was acquired by McDonalds Restaurants and is used as a Children's party bus in the Blackpool area. RM 1842 has been converted into a mobile caravan and sees occasional use.

RM 2103 was one of the first Routemasters to be sold by a former London Buses company and has been used around the United Kingdom undertaking work for the International Fund for Animal Welfare (IFAW). This vehicle is owned by a company by the name of Freight Media. In early 1996, they acquired RM 125, which is used by Mars to promote the Snickers chocolate bar in connection with their football sponsorship. It has been repainted in all-over green with football netting painted over the top. Internally it has been refitted to resemble a football pitch. It has been used since 1996 for the Euro '96 football competition and also the 1998 football World Cup as well as other Snickers promotional work. RM 2129 is also owned by Freight Media, having been acquired in August 1996, and this vehicle is the only one of the three to retain its seats.

The London Transport Central Distribution Services (CDS) subsidiary at Acton own RCL 2221 which is still available for hire. It is fitted out as an exhibition vehicle but has latterly been used as a travel information vehicle for London Transport. It was first used for the Shillibeer celebrations in 1979. RCL 2223 was extensively retrimmed in 1986 at London Transport's Aldenham works and included the fitment of 22 coach-type seats, a kitchen area, and a downstairs bar. With its luxury fittings, it was used as both a hospitality and promotional vehicle. It was subsequently refitted with a

Above **RMC 1496 was acquired by Sextons in 1994 and has been sent to various events including many sporting venues. It is here leaving Epsom Racecourse on Derby Day 5th June 1999.**
Alan Conway

RM 255 last operated with Stagecoach subsidiary United Counties at Bedford in September 1993, and after being stored, was sold in 1999 to a dealer. In 2000 it passed to Green Bohemia and is seen in its distinctive turquoise livery.
Geoff Rixon

demonstration area on the lower deck, including removable display units, television monitors and video facilities. It also has a bar and cold food cabinet, and kitchen, conference and eating area on the upper deck. RCL 2243 has been purchased by Medway FM Radio and is understood to be currently undergoing conversion for its new role. RCL 2226 and RCL 2238 have been used since their sale from London Buses as catering vehicles for the film industry. Former Magicbus RM 1145 was also used in this role from early 1995 until early 2000. RCL 2254 is privately owned but was used by Bus Engineering Ltd (BEL) for promotional work until early 1993, and remains in an all-over white livery.

Of the former Northern General vehicles, RCN 697 has been used by Coca-Cola since early 1998 as a promotional vehicle and is regularly seen on tour around the UK. The only other RMF in non-PSV use is FPT581C which is fitted out as a playbus.

Surprisingly, not many of the former British Airways RMA vehicles have seen non-PSV use. As these vehicles are fitted with doors as standard (as

RM 581 was converted to open top at London Transport's Aldenham works in 1985 and passed to Steven Austin Newspapers. It remains in use with this company and is seen in Waltham Cross High Street in March 1998.
John G.S. Smith

ROUTEMASTER HANDBOOK

Above and right
Since late 1999, BBC Television have been using RM 872 to promote 'beeb.com'. In autumn 2000 the bus appeared in a new white and blue based livery. On 14th October 2000 it is seen in Bromley town centre. This RM was sold in March 1998 after having last seen service with London Central on route 36.
Nigel Edon-Clarke

with the RMFs), they would have been a natural choice for this type of work. RMA 9 is the former Wembley Stadium courtesy vehicle and has been owned by a chain of estate agents since June 1999 and is used as a promotional vehicle for this company. RMA 53 continues to be available for hire as a hospitality bus. RMA 23 was used by Lever as a promotional vehicle, and had its staircase removed from the standard position and two staircases installed at the rear. However, it passed to an owner in the West Midlands area and is now believed to have been scrapped.

Above **RM 843** was owned for several years by television company Bravo. In it is seen parked at the American Car Museum near Uckfield in Sussex.
Andrew Short

Right **Former Magicbus and Kelvin Central RM 1274** is known as 'The Web Bus' and has been used since late 1995 as a mobile youth club in the Woking area in conjunction with Surrey County Council.
Graham Lunn

Above **RM 1790 has been owned by the London Borough of Lewisham since 1985 and continues in use as a playbus.**
Glyn Matthews

Below **Former Greater Manchester RM 1807 is seen in its latest livery at the McDonalds Restaurant in Mereside near Blackpool where it is used as a children's party bus.**
Glyn Matthews

Above **RM 1836**, along with the other buses owned by Andrew Boath, can be seen used for many types of promotional work. Open top RM 1836 was used by Chester Bus & Boat and Bryn Melyn Motors before being acquired by its present owner in 1997. In 1998, it was used for a promotion for Fox Kids.
Andrew Morgan

Right **RM 2178** has been owned by Fuzzy Duzzy Children's Entertainer since late 1998. It was repainted red shortly before being sold by its previous owner, having previously been in green and yellow livery as 'The Bio Garden Bus'.
Bob Martin

Right The rear door to RCL 2226 was fitted soon after its new life as a film location vehicle commenced in 1985. It is currently owned by Aeroshoot Film Services. Andrew Morgan

Below RCL 2218 has been owned and used as a playbus by the London Borough of Redbridge since 1985. It is seen at the 2000 North Weald rally when it appeared newly painted in this purple livery. Andrew Morgan

Above **RCL 2221 has been used since 1998 as a mobile information centre and was subsequently repainted into this new livery in 1999.** Geoff Rixon

Right **RCL 2238, like RCL 2226, is a film location vehicle fitted out with chairs and tables for use as a mobile canteen. In its latest livery, it is passing through Marble Arch in August 2000.** Geoff Rixon

Right **RMA 9 is seen with its third owner since used as a staff bus by Bus Engineering Ltd (BEL). It was sold by The Townends Group in October 2000 after use on promotional work.**
Geoff Rixon

Below **Former Northern General RCN 697 has been used by Coca-Cola on promotional work since 1998. In October 1999 it is seen in use in connection with the Rugby World Cup promotion.**
Andrew Morgan

RM 1 is seen out and about occasionally at rallies and other events and was photographed at Brooklands in April 1999. Andrew Morgan

Being the last London designed traditional open rear platform bus, large numbers of the popular Routemaster were natural candidates for the preservationist. All four prototypes survive today; RM 1 and RM 2 were donated to the London Transport Museum, Covent Garden, in March 1985, Leyland-engined RM 3 was sold to the London Bus Preservation Trust at Cobham in February 1974 and Leyland-engined RMC 4 passed to a private preservationist in early 2000. The unique front-entrance, rear engined Routemaster, FRM 1, was donated to the London Transport Museum in May 1984. Of these none are on permanent display, and only RM 2 was on display for a time when it was on long-term loan to the Oxford Bus Museum at Long Hanborough. RM 1 and RM 2 make rare appearances at rallies and FRM 1 was recertified for the Routemaster 40 celebrations in 1994. Since 1999, vehicles in the London Transport Museum collection which are not on display at Covent Garden museum are stored at 'The Depot' at Acton. This new facility is open to the public on selected dates throughout the year. Additionally,

RM 1562 and RM 2050, former London Transport Buses Reserve Fleet vehicles, are owned by the Friends of the London Transport Museum.

The number of Routemasters that have passed into preservation continues to increase every year and in October 2000 (excluding the prototypes) there were eighty-two RMs, eleven RMCs, ten RMAs, four RCLs and four RMFs preserved in one form or another in the United Kingdom. Of these, RCL 2229 and RM 1737 were donated to the London Transport Museum in April 1985 and January 1986 respectively. Since December 1993, RM 1737 has been on display at the London Transport Museum at Covent Garden. RM 1737 is also famous as the first ever all-over advert bus when in August 1969 it appeared in a livery for Silexine Paints. Initially vehicles (excluding the RMFs) were sold directly from London Transport and included a few of the former garage showbuses (e.g. RMs 8, 254, 737, 1000, 1563 and 2116). Of these RM 2116 is preserved in the '1933' livery that it gained in 1983 as part of the celebrations to commemorate fifty years of London Transport. RM 8 saw only nine years service with London Transport, after use as an experimental vehicle based at Chiswick works. It was saved for preservation initially by a group from the now defunct Sidcup garage. At the time of writing, former showbus RM 14 was undergoing restoration by the well known company that scrapped over 50 per cent of the RMs built. As it is now 18 years since sales commenced from London Transport, many buses have now had up to four or more owners. There are currently 18 Leyland-engined RMs preserved. Of the RMFs, only one retains a Leyland engine. Similarly, of the RMCs, prototype RMC 4 retains a Leyland engine, being the only one of the class so fitted. In 1987, RM 66 was cut down to a single-deck vehicle as a mock RM towing vehicle. Former Clydeside Scottish RM 110 is now owned by a custom car club and has been fully customised as detailed in the previous chapter. RM 1368 was uniquely converted to a single-deck

RM 66 was converted in 1987 to become a pseudo towing vehicle in the style of the STL conversions. It later passed to BTS Coaches of Borehamwood and was used as an engineering support unit alongside the RMLs on London Transport route 13 until 1995. It then passed to the 447 Group and is seen at the Cardiff rally in June 2000. Malcolm King

Routemaster by London Transport in 1975 and was used until 1989 by the Chiswick based experimental department. After being vandalised, then acquired by two dealers, it was finally secured for preservation in 1997.

Museums with Routemasters in their collections include Cobham Bus Museum with RM 3, St Helens Museum with RM 991 and RM 1152, Westgate Museum near Doncaster with RM 529, Aston Manor Road Transport Museum with RM 506, the Greater Manchester Museum with RM 1414, the Scottish Vintage Bus Museum at Lathalmond with RM 560, RM 606, RM 910 and RM 1607 and RMA 50, the Science Museum at Wroughton with RM 140 and BaMMOT at Wythall with RCL 2219. All of these vehicles are actually owned by individuals, with the exception of Stagecoach's vintage fleet at Lathalmond and Greater Manchester's RM 1414. The latter was donated by London Transport in January 1983.

Among all these vehicles, every example of London red livery is represented except the current versions. Generally, when Routemasters are acquired for preservation, they are returned to London red livery. Hence liveries such as Blackpool Transport, Kelvin Scottish, Strathtay Scottish or United Counties to name a few, have all disappeared. However, three vehicles are currently preserved in the former Clydeside Scottish livery. Examples have been sold from Stagecoach and Strathtay Scottish for preservation, but they have all reverted to the colours of their original owners. One example is RM 938 which has attended rallies in Europe on many occasions between May 1992 and 1999 including three rallies in the Czech Republic. It was the only Reading Mainline Routemaster to be repainted and retains this livery. Six former Southampton City Transport

Leyland engined RM 16 was one of the earliest Routemasters into preservation, from 1984 in fact. It is preserved in the livery it had when it left London service complete with white roundel and London Regional Transport legal lettering.
Andrew Morgan

vehicles have been preserved but only one retains its second owner's livery. Only one of the former Southend Transport RMs (1543) retains its blue and white livery. With the recent withdrawal of the Reading Mainline fleet, there are currently seven preserved Routemasters that retain this livery. RM 441 retains its distinctive red and yellow Black Prince livery. Open-top RM 1403, formerly owned by Allied Breweries, now carries LT red livery in preservation. This was the first RM converted to open-top configuration. RMs 54, 597, 759, 909, 910 and 1224 are currently preserved in liveries that Routemasters never actually carried in passenger service. RM 54 was repainted in Blackburn Corporation Transport livery in early 1994. Former Strathtay RM 759 was repainted in early 1993 to Glasgow Corporation livery complete with retrimmed seats in DMS style London blue moquette and green paintwork in lieu of the burgundy rexine and gloss paintwork. Former Magicbus RM 909 was repainted in early 1997 in the Western SMT livery of red and white. Former Kelvin RM 910 now carries its second livery with the Edinburgh Transport Group of Edinburgh Corporation livery; it had previously been repainted in a version of the Edinburgh tram livery. RM 2208 was restored in 1994 to the Shillibeer livery. Three of the RCLs that have been fully restored (i.e. RCLs 2219, 2229 and 2233) have been restored in the original Green Line livery, and of the preserved RMCs, five have been restored to original livery. The exceptions are RMC 1459 and RMC 1476 which received the 1970s National Bus Company leaf green colour scheme.

The former Northern General RMF fleet of 51 vehicles has declined drastically. Only four vehicles are preserved, including the original RMF 1254, which is slowly being restored to original as-built condition. From early 1992, Go Ahead Northern saw the occasional use of one of their

original fleet of RMFs, former Stagecoach EDS508B (formerly RCN699), now re-registered PCN762. Although it has now been fitted with an AEC engine and has lost its original registration, one would not realise that it had left the fleet some 15 years previously. It is actually owned by the GoAhead Northern Bus Enthusiast Association and is seen at shows and other special events. It was repainted in 1992 in a variation of its original livery of maroon and cream but with Northern fleet names.

Above **Former Stagecoach Magicbus and East Midland RM 909 was repainted in early 1997 into full Western SMT livery.**
Andrew Morgan

Right **RM 1224 was repainted in July 1998 in this livery with its front in half London and half Stagecoach Scotland colours.**
Andrew Morgan

The former British Airways RMA vehicles survive in reasonably large numbers with just over half of the class still in existence, but only a few are preserved. Two vehicles were restored to original BEA livery of mid-blue and white but of these only one remains preserved, this being BEA 1 (otherwise remembered as RMA 28). Additionally one was restored to the intermediate BEA livery of orange and white but this vehicle has since returned to passenger service with International Coachlines. RMA 6 is currently

Right RM 1368 reappeared at rallies in the summer of 1998 after an absence of nine years. This unique single deck Routemaster had been used from 1975 to 1989 by the London Transport experimental department at Chiswick works but was then severely damaged following vandalism in 1989. It was then sold to a dealer and is now privately preserved.
Andrew Morgan

Below RM 1403 was the first standard Routemaster to be converted to open top, albeit the first two were to a different style to those that followed for London Coaches. It was converted at Aldenham works in 1984 for use by Benskins Brewery which was part of Allied Breweries. In 1992 it passed to private ownership and in 1997 it was repainted from the Benskins maroon back to red livery.
Andrew Morgan

preserved in the BEL livery of grey and red. RMA 14 carries Green Rover livery, but it never actually carried this livery whilst in passenger service. The others are preserved in London Transport red. RMA 19 was rebuilt as a semi-preserved vehicle that could be used as a mobile caravan or hospitality vehicle, complete with shower and toilet. It has also been fitted with an RM type front blind box.

Right RMC 1469 was used by London United until 1995 as a recruitment vehicle; the interior of the vehicle has so far not been altered from this role. It was secured for preservation in 1998 and was acquired by its present owner the following year.
Andrew Morgan

Below RMC 1476 was used by London Transport and London Coaches as a training vehicle before passing into preservation in 1993. In 1997 it was repainted into National Bus Company leaf green livery and thus illustrated the period in its life when used by London Transport in this livery as a trainer.
Andrew Morgan

Right **RCL 2229 passed to the London Transport Museum in 1985 after use at Stamford Hill from 1980 to 1984. A thorough restoration followed, including repaint from red back to Green Line livery.**
Andrew Morgan

Below **Former Northern General RMF PCN762 was originally registered RCN699 and has subsequently operated for Stevensons of Uttoxeter and Magicbus in Glasgow. In 1992, it returned to its native home having been secured for preservation. It is seen a long way from its home at the North Weald rally in June 1997.**
Andrew Morgan

At the time of writing, there were 413 Routemasters outside the British Isles. With 378 of these being standard RMs, there are now more RMs overseas than are left in the United Kingdom. It was only natural that the Routemaster would follow the RT class and be bought by overseas customers wanting to own a real London bus. It should be remembered that large numbers of double-deckers including Bristol FLFs and even Bristol VRs have been repainted red and shipped abroad to masquerade as London buses! The first and a one-off export was RML 2691 for use by Mary Quant in Canada in 1972. This vehicle was found in 1998 and has been out of use in Sweden for a number of years.

From 1982, London Buses vehicles became available and straight away four standard RMs were exported in August 1982 to the Karuizawa Classic Car Museum in Japan. Unusually, RM 1248 was exported without an engine with the intention of being used as a static display. Since then, in total three hundred and seventy eight RMs, nine RCLs, one RML, ten RMCs, four RMFs and eleven RMAs have departed from the United Kingdom for forty-seven different countries around the world.

RMA 22 is one of three former London Coaches RMAs to find a new home in Ireland. It was acquired by J.J. Kavanagh & Sons of Kilkenny in early 1995.
Andrew Morgan

Above **RM 2077 is seen in La Plata in Argentina in July 2000 where it is used on a cultural tour of the city. La Plata is the provincial capital of Buenos Aires Province and is approximately 40 miles (64km) from Buenos Aires city.**
Paul Crossland

ARGENTINA (total 15 RMs)

| RM | 89, | 104, | 172, | 317, | 621, | 698, | 790, | 969, | 982, | 1017, | 1070, | 1136, |
| | 1266, | 2046, | 2077. | | | | | | | | | |

The most recent continent to see the influx of numerous Routemasters is South America, most notably in Argentina. Three RMs have been seen during 2000 at Parque de la Costa near Buenos Aires and RM 2077 is used on a tour of the city of La Plata. However, reports of most of the other vehicles are sketchy.

Right **RM 1070 is seen operating a service to the amusement park by the name of Parque de la Costa in Tigre, which is the northern suburb of Buenos Aires in Argentina.**
Paul Crossland

RM 1708 has been in Australia since August 1988 but is now being restored by its new owners at the Bus & Truck Museum at Tempe in Sydney.
Chris O'Brien

AUSTRALIA (total 1 RM)

| RM | 1708. |

RM 1708 was used as a school bus in Perth in Western Australia but passed to the Bus & Truck Museum at Tempe in Sydney in October 1998 where it joined RT 3708.

AUSTRIA (total 2 RMs)

| RM | 416, | 751. |

RM 416 is a static children's party bus outside a McDonald's Restaurant.

RM 416 was well known when operating with Clydeside Scottish, subsequently going to East Yorkshire in Hull. In December 1997, it is seen in a suburb of Innsbruck at Rum as another children's party bus. Brian Goulding

Former Clydeside Scottish RM 859 is used by Ceremonie Roger in Meulebeke in Belgium. Of note are the chrome wheel trims front and rear and the platform door. Roger Eeckhout

BELGIUM (total 21 RMs, 2 RCLs, 1 RMF)

RM	206,	209,	234,	305,	494,	625,	812,	859,	944,	977,	1006,	1088,
	1428,	1555,	1684,	1711,	1731,	1732,	1791,	1825,	1897.			
RCL	2245,	2250.										
RMF	FPT580C.											

In 1983, De Dubbeldekkers based near Antwerp in Belgium acquired a number of RMs. However, some have since disappeared without trace. McDonalds Restaurants have acquired at least two RMs. The two RCLs listed are used on promotional work by Corona. Both remain on British registration plates; RCL 2250 was even seen back in England at the beginning of 2000 for an engine change.

Former Clydeside Scottish RM 234 is seen at Aalst in Belgium in June 1999 having now been converted to open-top for its new rôle. Maurice Bateman

Right **RM 206** is seen in March 1997 being used as a hospitality vehicle. It is one of the many Routemasters to have been exported and disappeared, only to have been located several years later. Maurice Bateman

Below **RM 625** has been owned by Aspekt Mobiel since June 1997. It was converted to open top for its last operational use in the British Isles as part of the Chester Bus & Boat Tour. It is seen at a show in Belgium in July 2000. K Van Camp

Right RM 209 was converted to open top but since this photograph was taken it has had the roof rebuilt. It was being used as a fish and chip shop when seen at Vrasene in Belgium.
Maurice Bateman

Below RM 1732 now has a platform door and a flat roof which is seen in the raised position n July 1997 after being repainted into Dorito's promotional livery.
Philip Roisin

RM 1314 has been used since July 1999 in Bermuda to transport guests up the hill from Cross Bay beach to the Sonesta Hotel. It was converted to open top before leaving the British Isles.
Brian Northcott

BERMUDA (total 1 RM)

RM	1314.

RM 1314 sees use carrying tourists staying at the Sonestra Hotel.

BULGARIA (total 1 RM)

RM	1366.

CANADA (total 39 RMs, 2 RCLs)

RM	113,	187,	318,	504,	583,	663,	794,	797,	937,	986,	1072,	1102,
	1221,	1242,	1371,	1415,	1424,	1448,	1548,	1604,	1618,	1620,	1651,	1676,
	1752,	1773,	1788,	1888,	1904,	1909,	1924,	1943,	1950,	2133,	2162,	2165,
	2174,	2206,	2209.									
RCL	2252,	2255.										

Operators in Canada were quick to acquire former London Buses Routemasters and currently Double Deck Tours at Niagara Falls own sixteen RMs and two RCLs, Capital Double Deck & Trolley Tours (formerly known as Piccadilly Bus Tours) at Ottawa own six RMs, London Picadilly (yes, they do spell it this way) Buses at Tottenham operate two RMs (but they are actually owned by two different companies), Abegweit Tours in Charlottetown own two RMs, Royal Blue Line Tours own a former Burnley & Pendle RM as well as a former preserved RM which is now open top, and the Duke of Kent Bus Tours in Ontario own one RM for charter work. Double Deck Tours have been undertaking a programme to fit custom made platform doors to the Routemaster fleet, with six completed by August 2000 including both RCLs. RM 504 and RM 2209 were acquired by Double Deck Tours from Beach Bus Company in August 1997 as open top vehicles; RM 2209 was repainted in 1998 and is used for charter work only. RM 797 is in a special livery for the shuttle bus from Niagara Falls to Niagara-on-the-Lake which commenced in April 1998. RM 794 was covered with approximately 100,000 gold coloured pre-decimal pennies. For several years it operated a shuttle between the Skylon Tower and the Imax Theatre, but is now out of use. Former McDonalds playbus RM 1924 operates as London Bus Tours in Burlington, Ontario and retains its McDonalds interior. Open top RM 504 was sold in June 2000 to the 1000 Islands Ganonoque Chamber of Commerce and is used to operate the first transit service in Canada to be operated entirely by a double-decker bus. It is planned that the normal months of operation will be the middle of May to early October.

Above **Double Deck Tours RCL 2252 is seen in the new livery in June 1998.** George Gamblin

Right **Double Deck Tours RM 1651 was rebuilt with the roof from an RTW after a roof accident. If you look carefully, you can see different internal light fittings and a lack of poles from the seat frames to the roof.** George Gamblin

Above **Former Southend Transport and Beach Bus RM 797 is the first Double Deck Tours Routemaster to be given a special livery. It is seen at the Niagara-on-the-Lake stand in June 1998 awaiting its next journey on the shuttle service. A common feature of Double Deck Tours operations is their use** with the upper deck emergency window in the open position.
George Gamblin

Below **Double Deck Tours acquired open top** RM 2209 from Beach Bus Company in North Carolina in 1997 and, after a repaint in 1998, it entered service but on charters only.
Bob Martin

Above **RM 2133 with Royal Blue Line Motor Tours in British Columbia is typical of many Routemasters outside the British Isles which have retained** their non-London blinds; in this case the Burnley and Pendle Eastender blinds which are still displayed.
Bob Martin

Below **Royal Blue Line acquired RM 113 in 1996 but it suffered roof damage in transit and was subsequently converted to open top.**
Bob Martin

Top RM 2174 is seen operating a shuttle service in North Bay, Ontario whilst on hire from London Picadilly Buses to North Bay Transit in August 2000. This vehicle was originally to be exported to Japan but five years later was sold to Beach Bus Company in North Carolina. It subsequently passed to London Picadilly Buses in Tottenham, Ontario in 1994 where it still operates at the time of writing. Paul Bateson

Centre RM 1924 is seen visiting Niagara Falls in September 1999 with Double Deck Tours RMs parked in front. The rear platform has been raised and the platform pole moved rearwards to allow the wheel chair ramp (which is housed under the two steps) to be pulled out. Also visible is the rear door which is seen folded in the open position where the used ticket bin is normally visible. Gord Welham

Bottom RM 504 was acquired in June 2000 to operate in the town of Gananoque on the shuttle service. This is a transit route, complete with bus stops which depict an open top Routemaster, rather than a sightseeing tour. RM 504 is seen on 3rd August 2000. Paul Bateson

Above RM 1773 was converted to open top in March 1995 and is seen in Ottawa in July 2000. Capital Double Decker & Trolley Tours were previously known as Piccadilly Bus Tours (not to be confused with London Picadilly Buses). Peter Coney

Below RM 1943 and RM 1788 are seen in their depot and have been operating in Ottawa since export from London in 1986. Noteworthy is the new style livery with the new Capital Double Decker & Trolley Tours fleet names. Peter Coney

Former East Yorkshire RM 798 was exported to the Czech Republic in April 2000 and is seen operating a special service linking Chlumec with Usti nad Labem fire station on 27th May 2000. David Griffiths

CZECH REPUBLIC (total 4 RMs, 1 RMA)

RM	527,	798,	1013,	1176.
RMA	15.			

CROATIA – SEE FORMER YUGOSLAVIA (total 1 RM)

DENMARK (total 2 RMs)

RM	755,	1086.

EIRE (total 2 RMs, 3 RMAs)

RM	406,	2005.	
RMA	22,	25,	26.

Former Southend Transport RM 2005 and former London Coaches RMA 25 and RMA 26 are operated by Dualway Coaches and were used at first on their sightseeing services in Dublin. RM 406 also joined this fleet late in 1999 having been owned by Irish Commercials at Naas since November 1992. Currently, apart from RMA 25, the use of these vehicles is limited to private

hire work. RMA 25 was converted to open-top in 1995 and was the first RMA to be so converted. It has been used to operate on a tour of Kilkenny, Ireland's smallest city, during the summer months. J.J. Kavanagh of Urlingford own former London Coaches RMA 22 which is used primarily for private hire work.

Above **RM 2005 has been with Dualway based near Dublin since 1994, having previously operated with Southampton City Transport and Southend Transport. It was repainted from blue and white to this burgundy and silver based livery several years ago and is nowadays used for special duties instead of sightseeing work.**
Andrew Morgan

Right **RMA 25 was the first RMA to be converted to open top. For the 1999 summer season, it operated for Dualway in Kilkenny and, after the end of the season, in September, it was used by J.J. Kavanagh in connection with Kilkenny's appearance in the final of the All Ireland Hurling championship.**
Andrew Morgan

FINLAND (total 5 RMs, 1 RMA, 1 RMF)

RM	421,	584,	626,	826,	1077.
RMA	10.				
RMF	FPT591C.				

FRANCE (total 24 RMs, 5 RMCs, 3 RMAs)

RM	48,	53,	58,	102,	226,	339,	359,	459,	552,	611,	696,	702,
	781,	1041,	1133,	1425,	1585,	1609,	1681,	1810,	1912,	2032,	2041,	2200.
RMC	1458,	1488,	1499,	1503,	1519.						
RMA	17,	20,	56.								

Open top RM 102 has been used since Easter 2000 in Paris by the Parisian river cruises operator Bateaux Mouches, and is in a black livery. Most RMs are used for various tourist or promotional uses. Open top RM 339 is owned by The Imperial Red Ltd who are based in Toulouse. However, this RM is believed to now be for sale.

Above **RMC 1499 is now used as an accommodation vehicle at the Route de Taxo Kart Circuit at Argeles sur Mer in France. This RMC has been in France since 1991 although it is now with its second owner. The London United fleet names are reminders of its days as a trainer at Hounslow and Shepherds Bush between 1987 and 1991.** Linda Simmonds

Right **RM 1681 was a take-away pizza restaurant near Toulouse in south France when seen in November 1998.** Graham Lunn collection

RM 470 was sold by London Buses in late 1994 and passed straight to Hermann-Josef Hertfurtner in Dusseldorf. The open top conversion reduces the overall height to under 4.0m. It is seen being used on a promotion for a newspaper.
Hermann-Josef Hertfurtner

GERMANY (total 26 RMs, 2 RMCs)

RM	88,	98,	149,	335,	444,	470,	546,	550,	555,	641,	709,	832,
	1047,	1054,	1111,	1181,	1212,	1682,	1758,	1815,	1882,	1883,	1947,	2101,
	2120,	2212.										
RMC	1481,	1486.										

Twenty-six Routemasters, including two RMCs, have gone to Germany. Again most have been put to use in various promotional roles including RM 88 which is a mobile pub for Heidelberger. There are at least four RMs for McDonalds in Germany in use as children's static party buses. RM 470 is another typical example; upstairs it had some of the seats turned around to face one another with tables fitted between and it has been converted to open top. A flat canvas roof is fitted to keep the vehicle weathertight and to maintain its overall height at under 4.0 metres. Downstairs, a similar layout has been fitted but a bar and fridge have been fitted on the right hand side in place of the bench seat. It is used for promotional work, on tours, at fairs and at private parties.

GREECE (total 1 RM)

RM	1991.

HONG KONG (total 2 RMs)

RM	1288,	1873.

Perhaps the most bizarre adaptation of bodywork for a new use is in Hong Kong. In 1984, RMs 1288 and 1873 were exported in the hope that further orders from China would be forthcoming. In the late 1980s, they were

ROUTEMASTER HANDBOOK

rebuilt by Citybus, complete with mock wooden seats and open staircases in the approximate style of London buses in the 1920s. The only recognisable features of these vehicles are the cabs and wheels ! Both are now in standard Citybus yellow and red livery and are used for private hire and contract work. In the summer of 1991, two further vehicles arrived in the Colony. One of these was former Clydeside Scottish RM 1703 which was converted to open top and painted maroon; this vehicle was scrapped late in 1999 after not being used for some time. A fourth Routemaster was acquired, RM 870, but was not used and was later dismantled.

Facing page
Hong Kong Citybus RM 1288 – close up of platform and steps.
Andrew Morgan

Above **RM 1288 at Hong Kong Citybus's Fo Tan depot in January 1999.**
Andrew Morgan

HUNGARY (total 8 RMs)

| RM | 788, | 1417, | 1649, | 1911, | 2087, | 2100, | 2114, | 2205. |

IRAQ (total 1 RM)

| RM | 1134. |

ITALY (total 11 RMs)

| RM | 154, | 264, | 346, | 413, | 713, | 732, | 769, | 956, | 1109, | 1359, | 1433. |

Of the eleven vehicles in Italy, RM 1433 was converted to transport a motorcycle and is now partially open top. Iveco engined RM 346 is used by a promotional company in Milan and returns to England every year for servicing!

Three former Southampton City Transport RMs are used by the Koyama Driving school in Kanagawa in Japan as waiting rooms. Two are in this light blue livery and one is painted dark blue. This RM is thought to be RM 2043.

Graham Lunn collection

JAPAN (total 45 RMs)

RM												
	109,	204,	286,	312,	326,	496,	564,	592,	600,	632,	638,	715,
	785,	820,	851,	943,	1090,	1131,	1154,	1187,	1192,	1248,	1251,	1339,
	1384,	1404,	1539,	1546,	1549,	1619,	1713,	1730,	1793,	1796,	1819,	1889,
	2018,	2026,	2043,	2113,	2131,	2145,	2150,	2166,	2193.			

There had been the possibility of a large number of Routemasters being exported to Japan for use as burger bars, but this enquiry fell through in 1989 and only small batches of them were exported there. Despite this, Japan still boasts the largest number of Routemasters outside the UK. Many of them have been used as mobile shops or restaurants, parked at various locations from time to time. Unfortunately, they were usually sold to an agent in the UK who sold them to a Japanese agent who in turn would pass them to their new owner. This system, together with the usual difficulties with the language barrier, resulted in very little information being returned to their homeland.

RM 1192 was being used as a pub when found in February 1997 at Tenjin in Fukuoka City in Japan. The platform door arrangement is certainly very unusual.
Graham Lunn collection

KENYA (total 4 RMs)

| RM | 516, | 1170, | 1257, | 2187. |

The most recent vehicles to be exported to the continent of Africa are to Kenya where they are used for staff transport from local villages to farms in Naivasha.

LEBANON (total 1 RM)

| RM | 457. |

RM 457, was exported to Beirut in 1985 for use by a fashion boutique but was last reported as being used to ferry guests between a palace and a race course in the Bekkaa Valley!

RM	1180.

RM 1180 is preserved and is often seen in use with events in connection with the Tramways and Bus Museum of the City of Luxembourg. It was originally exported for a British trade fair in October 1991 with the intention of returning back to London. However, an offer was made to purchase the RM and it was sold by London Buses.

RM 1180 is seen in Luxembourg about to depart on a road run in May 1998 to commemorate the 90th anniversary of the original Luxembourg bus route.
Andrew Morgan

MEXICO (total 6 RMs)

RM   512,   735,   946,   1068,   1647,   2003.

Three RMs were exported by London Buses to Cancun in Mexico and are used to promote night clubs and a hotel. RM 946 was static in Mexico City whilst RM 735 and RM 2003 carry holidaymakers from the Krystal Hotel and La Boom night club in Cancun on the Caribbean coast. They were joined at Cancun by three former Stagecoach United Counties RMs in late 1999.

Three former Stagecoach United Counties RMs were exported to Mexico in late 1999 where they joined the three that were acquired directly from London service in 1994. All six are used in connection with La Boom nightclub in Cancun. RM 735 is seen in the background with its partial open top conversion with the front and rear roof domes still intact.
Paul Crossland

RM 43 was converted
to open top before
leaving the British Isles
and is used by
Kooy Laminations at
Aalsmeer in the
Netherlands.
Jan vd Stelt

THE NETHERLANDS (total 9 RMs)

RM	43,	682,	718,	757,	924,	1149,	1156,	1163,	2124.

NEW ZEALAND (total 3 RMs)

RM	221,	1660,	1670.

In New Zealand, RM 1660 is used as a mail bus by operating two 30-mile
return trips each day and RM 1670 is used as a tour bus in Auckland. By
November 1996, RM 1670 had had its Leyland 0600 engine replaced with a
Hino EK100 unit. Former Strathtay RM 221 is owned by aviation enthusiast
Sir Tim Wallis and is open top. It is confined to Wanaka airfield where it has
been used as a hamburger bar.

NORWAY (total 5 RMs)

RM	223,	232,	549,	828,	1887.

Out of the RMs in Norway, two are out of use, one is preserved and the
remaining two are in use by the welfare club of Halden Trafikk who are based
in eastern Norway.

OMAN (total 1 RM)

RM	2171.

RM 2171 and RM 2183 were shipped to Oman for a British Festival in 1989
and found new owners in the area; RM 2183 was then sold to an owner in the
United Arab Emirates.

PARAGUAY (total 1 RM)

RM	1545.

Right RM 1660 was exported to New Zealand in 1986 and, after use on tours between Queenstown and Arrowtown, it has most recently been reported in use as a post bus on a twice daily 30-mile route. Colin Stannard

Below RM 1670 has been in New Zealand for some 16 years. In December 1998, it is seen in Auckland with some incredible wheel trims. Trevor Muir

POLAND (total 15 RMs, 1 RMC)

RM	219,	321,	364,	398,	438,	706,	824,	879,	949,	1053,	1700,	1741,
	1948,	1983,	2024.									
RMC	1492.											

In August 1999, an advertising agency in Warsaw acquired six RMs and one RMC. All were used until the end of 1999 on a contract for the Norwich Union to promote pensions. RM 364 was used from 1995 until late 1999 on promotions across Poland.

Facing page **Six RMs and a single RMC were used in the summer of 1999 by an advertising agency based in Warsaw in Poland. Initially they were used for a contract for the Norwich Union to advertise pensions. Former CentreWest recruitment vehicle RMC 1492 is seen in Warsaw in December 1999.** Alex Dyba

Above **RM 1700 is seen at Blaszki in Poland. It has been used since early 1999 as a promotional vehicle for Pietrucha SiA.** Alex Dyba

Right **The converted interior of RM 1700 is just recognisable as a Routemaster.** Alex Dyba

Stagecoach Portugal
RMA 8 is seen awaiting
its inaugural journey in
October 1998 at São
Pedro de Sintra before
departing for Ribeira
tram terminus. The
unusual open top
conversion on this and
RMA 5 was carried out
in England by Kent
Coachworks and they
were repainted at
Stagecoach East
London's Leyton
garage.
Mario António Lido

PORTUGAL (total 2 RMs, 2 RMAs)

RM	81,	1271.
RMA	5,	8.

RMA 5 and RMA 8 arrived with Stagecoach Portugal from England by boat in April 1998 after conversion and repaint by their former operator, Stagecoach East London. They were both converted to open top and had their entrance moved from the left hand side to the right hand side behind the fuel filler. After repairs and certification work, they entered service on 1st October 1998 for the end of the 1998 season and have been used for the subsequent summer seasons.

Although technically in Portugal, RM 81 and RM 1271 are in Madeira and were operated in Funchal by Lido Bus Tours. These two open-top RMs were used on a tour of the island but have been out of regular use since the end of the 1998 season. The platform was panelled over and entrance doors were fitted ahead of the rear axle on the same side as the driver's cab.

Right RMA 5 shows its unusual open top conversion, rear lights, registration plate position and re-positioned entrance/exit on the right hand side.
Peter Gascoine

Below RM 81 and RM 1271 are seen at the Casino Park Hotel in Funchal in Madeira. They were converted to open top and rebuilt with panelled in platform and doors on the same side as the driver's cab before leaving the British Isles. They operated from 1996 to 1998 under the name Lido Bus Tours, but have rarely operated subsequently.
Alan Morgan

RUSSIA (total 1 RM)

RM	342.

SAUDIA ARABIA (total 1 RM)

RM	521.

RM 521 was exported to Riyadh via the United Arab Emirates early in 1991 as a promotional vehicle for Mars Confectionery

SLOVENIA – *SEE FORMER YUGOSLAVIA* (total 3 RMs)

SOUTH AFRICA (total 2 RMs)

RM	1885,	1918.

SPAIN (total 14 RMs, 1 RMC, 2 RCLs, 1 RMF)

RM	1026,	1117,	1166,	1205,	1316,	1526,	1531,	1630,	1694,	1916,	1930,	1959,
	1988,	2081.										
RMC	1515.											
RCL	2235,	2256.										
RMF	FPT589C.											

Former London Coaches convertible open top RCL 2235 is seen with its new owner in Spain whilst undertaking a promotion for Alcatel.
Maurice Bateman collection

The next Routemaster to find an owner abroad, after the four to Japan in 1982, was former Northern General RMF FPT589C shipped to Spain in 1983 for promotional work. RM 1630 and RM 1930 are on the Canary Islands, rather than mainland Spain.

The front of RM 2155 was dramatically rebuilt some seven years ago when it was fitted with an Ashok engine in Sri Lanka. It is seen in December 1997 in Maharagama.
George Wright

SRI LANKA (total 41 RMs)

RM											
152,	194,	283,	327,	333,	344,	435,	499,	596,	649,	730,	731,
746,	800,	852,	1029,	1067,	1080,	1115,	1121,	1150,	1160,	1165,	1243,
1294,	1336,	1364,	1401,	1413,	1530,	1581,	1827,	1851,	1986,	2049,	2088,
2092,	2155,	2158,	2160,	2207.							

Outside the UK, most Routemasters are used for hospitality, promotional use or tourist services in one form or another with the exception of Sri Lanka. The Sri Lanka Transport Board acquired forty-one Routemasters via the Crown Commissioners as part of an international aid package. Following a re-organisation of the nationalised Regional Transport Boards in about 1990/91, each depot became a separate subsidiary company in its own right, and these companies were known as '. . . Peopolised Transport Company'. Because this scheme failed to achieve the aims sought, the 'peopolised' companies were merged into eleven larger companies in 1997. Disposals of the RMs had commenced by this time, and whilst several have passed to private owners, it is thought that some may have been scrapped. However, the latest report in September 1999 indicates that at least five remained in regular service, but there are probably others in use in other parts of the island.

All but RM 344 and RM 1165 have been traced since arrival in Sri Lanka and it is known that a second RM was at Wennappuwa depot. One as yet unidentified RM is now used as a static cricket score board at the Transport's sports ground in Colombo.

RM1029 leaves
Negombo bus station in
Sri Lanka for
Kockchikade on service
909 in September 1999
whilst a Duple Metsec
bodied Tata rests in the
sun behind. Matt Giles

ROUTEMASTER HANDBOOK

RM 327 awaits
departure on a school
run in Negombo bus
station. The bonnet and
grille are raised to
accommodate the
Ashok engine and also a
five-speed manual
gearbox. Matt Giles

During 1998, RML 2691 was located in Sweden. In March 1999 it is seen at the country and western theme park at Hillerstorp. This was the RML that was sold in 1972 to Gala Cosmetics for use by Mary Quant and completed tours of Canada and Finland before going missing for a time. Graham Lunn

SWEDEN (total 8 RMs, 1 RMC, 1 RML, 1 RMF, 1 RMA)

RM	192,	354,	498,	699,	809,	868,	918,	1701.
RMC	1480.							
RML	2691.							
RMF	RCN689.							
RMA	16.							

RML 2691 was located in poor condition at Hillerstorp in south west Sweden. Former Northern General RMF RCN689 is in Gothenburg and is used as a fish and chip shop under the name London Bus Catering. RM 809 and RMA 16 are owned by private owners and are used primarily on contract and private hire work.

Above **Former Clydeside Scottish SRMA 1 and London & Country RMA 16 has been owned by J C Omnibus since 1998 and is now based in southern Sweden.**
Jörgen Carlsson

Right **RCN 689 is used as a Fish and Chip shop and trades under the name London Bus Catering. It is seen in Gothenburg in Sweden in March 1999.**
Graham Lunn

SWITZERLAND (total 3 RMs)

RM	55,	720,	1197.

TURKEY (total 3 RMs)

RM	32,	905,	1282.

UKRAINE (total 1 RM)

RM	2192.

Former Stagecoach United Counties RM 2192 was exported to the Ukraine in April 1999 as part of the BBC Television's 'Children in Need' appeal where it was to take up duties as a playbus for local children.

UNITED ARAB EMIRATES (total 1 RM)

RM	2183.

URUGUAY (total 2 RMs)

RM	1740,	1951.

The pair were seen operating a free service at the resort of Punte del Este during the summer months of December to March.

UNITED STATES OF AMERICA (total 24 RMs)

RM	47,	87,	395,	447,	525,	598,	599,	951,	963,	1061,	1078,	1087,
	1158,	1313,	1611,	1754,	1756,	1843,	1949,	1969,	2002,	2010,	2152,	2181.

RM 47 is based at St Thomas in the Caribbean in the United States Virgin Islands. RM 87 and RM 1087 are currently for sale, after operating during 1999 for British Bus of Florida on the Miami City Tour. RM 1158 was rebuilt before export with the platform on the right hand side and the staircase on the left hand side and is now open top; however the exact ownership details for this vehicle are not clear. RM 951 and RM 963 are both preserved by their new owners.

RM 47, with numerically the first production body B5, is seen at St Thomas in the Caribbean in the summer of 1999.
Victoria Maybury

Former Clydeside Scottish RM951 is seen at the late 19th century Hill County Court House on Hillsboro Texas. The route 37 blinds are a tribute to its days as a garage showbus whilst at Clapton Garage in the early 1980s.
A. Mann

RM 963 is seen at the All British Field Meet at Marymore Park in Redmond in July 1999. It has been with its present owner since 1997, having had two previous owners since its sale from London Buses in 1988.
Janet Foley

Above Former White Rose Coaches Iveco engined RM 598 was exported to California in 1995 and converted to this unusual open top design along with sister vehicle RM 395.
Bob Martin

Below RM 2181 was retained by CentreWest after privatisation until April 1995 and then was sold to the British Bus Company in San Diego of California. It was converted to open top by its new owner.
Peter Coney

ROUTEMASTER HANDBOOK

Above **RM 87 and open-top RM 1087 were exported to Miami at the end of 1998 and were used during the following season by British Bus of Florida on the Miami City Tour. However, they have not been used subsequently and at the time of writing were for sale.**
George Gamblin

Right **Close up of RM 87 front upper deck windows.**
George Gamblin

WEST AFRICA (total 1 RM)

RM	1157.

YUGOSLAVIA (total 6 RMs)

RM	83,	995,	1020,	1522,	1720,	1917.

Unfortunately, contact with the four RMs in the former Yugoslavia has been lost and their current condition is unknown. RMs 1522, 1720 and 1917 are in the part of Yugoslavia which is now Slovenia. RM 1020 has been exported to Croatia for limited promotional use.

ZIMBABWE (total 1 RM)

RM	2063.

Former East Midland RM 2063, which remains in its green and silver livery, is used to transport old age pensioners from Harare to Borrowdale village in Zimbabwe to receive free tea and scones at the owner's restaurant.

In Illinois in the USA, RM 1313 is used as Quincy's own London Tour Bus by the Quincy Convention and Visitors Bureau. The hand painted fleet numbers match the British registration but are of course incorrect.
D. Bedford

At the time of writing, there were also ten RMs and three RCLs that are known to have been exported from the British Isles but no further details have been found. Unfortunately these details have not been made available by the various dealers and for further reports we are reliant on them being found in a particular country. The missing vehicles are as follows:

RM	648,	799,	837,	933,	1171,	1283,	1421,	1727,	2136,	2153.
RCL	2240,	2241,	2259.							

Two unidentified RMs have been seen in Hungary and Argentina and may be those identified in the following list as having unknown owners. They are a standard RM with McDonald's Restaurants at Bekasmegyer, Hungary, and a standard RM with 'Taller 4' in Buenos Aires.

Routemasters in existence at December 2000

Unlisted vehicles are believed to have been scrapped. The last known registration is listed.

RM	Registration	Present owner	Engine	Notes
1	SLT56	London Transport Museum	AEC	preserved, at Acton 'depot'
2	SLT57	London Transport Museum	AEC	preserved, at Acton 'depot'
3	SLT58	London Bus Preservation Trust, Cobham	Leyland	preserved, Leyland engine
5	VLT5	Arriva London North – Clapton	AEC	
6	VLT6	Arriva London South – Brixton	Iveco	
7	VLT7	Mr N. Hurley, Goole	AEC	preserved but never rallied
8	VLT8	RM8 Group, Sidcup	AEC	preserved
9	VLT9	London Central – New Cross	Scania	
10	XFF258	Mr A. Boath, Norwood Green	AEC	promotional vehicle
14	OYM424A	PVS, Barnsley	AEC	preserved
16	VLT16	Messrs B Lewer & T Potter, Watford	Leyland	preserved
17	WLT675	Mr A. Harlott, Ipswich	AEC	preserved
23	JFO256	London Bus Services Ltd	AEC	in storage
24	VLT24	Mr C.J. Kilby, Wimborne	AEC	preserved, occasional psv use, t/a Route 24
25	VLT25	Arriva London South – Brixton	Iveco	
29	OYM453A	Unknown owner, London	AEC	possibly an Internet café
32	XYJ428	Sanayi Ticaret, Izmir, Turkey	AEC	
40	VLT40	RM40 Group, London E12	AEC	preserved
43	BE-16-50	Mr J. Kruining, Kooy Laminations BV, Aalsmeer, The Netherlands	AEC	open top
44	VLT44	Mr S. Miles, Benfleet	AEC	preserved, Transmatic lighting fitted
45	AST415A	London Bus Services Ltd.	AEC	in storage, LT fitted fluorescent lighting upstairs only
47	GVS492	Mr Taylor, Charlotte Amalie, St Thomas, US Virgin Islands	AEC	static snack bar
48	LDS199A	Mr B. Medni, Hayange (57), France	AEC	Restaurant bus
53	OYM582A	Unknown owner, France	Iveco	location and use unknown
54	LDS279A	Mr S. Holmes, Blackburn	AEC	preserved in Blackburn Corporation livery
55	YVS289	Bussilibus SRL, Balerna, Switzerland	AEC	
58	9149SQ72	Le Musée de L'Auto, Le Mans (72), France	AEC	
66	VLT66	447 Group, Pontardawe, Swansea	AEC	preserved, converted to single-deck in 1987
70	VLT70	Mr A. Boath, Norwood Green	AEC	in storage
80	JSJ748	Arriva Presenting London – Wandsworth	AEC	rebuilt and reclassified ERM in 1990, re-numbered to ERM 48 in 1999
81	29-67-MD	Cabriolet Cars, Funchal, Madeira, Portugal	AEC	registered central offside door fitted and platform panelled over, open top, out of use
83	VLT83	Mr Z. Keric, Belgrade, Yugoslavia	AEC	condition unknown
84	JSJ747	Arriva Presenting London – Wandsworth	AEC	rebuilt and reclassified ERM in 1990, re-numbered to ERM 47 in 1999
85	VLT85	Blue Triangle, Rainham, Essex	AEC	former promotional vehicle, for sale
87	VLT87	Mr E. Riccombeni, Miami, Florida, USA	AEC	for sale, open top
88	OYM432A	Heidelberg Pilsner Brewery, Germany	AEC	promotional vehicle
89	CDQ721	Parque de la Costa, Tigre, Buenos Aires, Argentina	Iveco	promotional vehicle
90	JSJ746	Arriva Presenting London – Wandsworth	AEC	rebuilt & reclassified ERM in 1990, re-numbered to ERM 46 in 1999
94	JSJ749	Arriva Presenting London – Wandsworth	AEC	rebuilt & reclassified ERM in 1990, re-numbered to ERM 49 in 1999
98	FR JS 170	SudbadenBus GMBH, Freiburg, Germany	AEC	rebuilt with staircase on the left hand side and the platform on the right hand side
102	VLT102	Bateaux Mouches, Paris, France	AEC	open top
104	LDS280A	Paranacam, Parana City, Entre Rios Province, Argentina	AEC	refurbished by BTS in 1994, promotional vehicle

RM	Registration	Present owner	Engine	Notes
108	VLT108	Mr S. Lowings, Nottingham	Leyland	preserved
109	VLT109	Unisupply Co Ltd, Kanagawa, Japan	AEC	Dining bus
110	RSK572	Smoke City Wheelers, Tottenham	AEC	customised in 1992, Transmatic lighting fitted by Western in 1989
111	VLT111	Blue Triangle, Rainham, Essex	AEC	in storage
113	8054BR	Royal Blue Line Motor Tours, Victoria, Canada	AEC	open top
116	VLT116	Mr T. Nicholson, Chippenham	AEC	preserved, air suspension fitted by LT in 1980
120	SSL809	First Capital (920) – Hackney Wick	AEC	open top
121	SSL806	London Bus Services Ltd	AEC	in storage
125	VVS373	Freight Media, Paddington	AEC	promotional vehicle
140	VLT140	Mr R.C. Gale, Avonwick	AEC	preserved
143	VLT143	Arriva Presenting London – Wandsworth	AEC	rebuilt & reclassified ERM in 1990
149	EDS117A	Unknown owner, Dusseldorf, Germany	AEC	use unknown
152	60 6613	Colombo Metropolitan Bus Company Ltd, Sri Lanka - Ratmanlana depot (RL4)	AEC	
154	KGJ133A	Oliviera, Siracusa, Sicily, Italy	AEC	
158	VLT158	Mr B. Simmons, Stevenage	AEC	preserved
163	VLT163	Arriva Presenting London – Wandsworth	AEC	rebuilt & reclassified ERM in 1990
172	WYJ857	Unknown owner, Argentina	AEC	Transmatic lighting fitted by Southend Transport in 1988, location and use unknown
180	XVS830	London Bus Services Ltd.	AEC	in storage
187	ZD3993	Double Deck Tours (21), Niagara Falls, Ontario, Canada	—	Transmatic lighting fitted by Western in 1989, not used in service since acquisition, engine removed, store shed
188	VLT188	East Yorkshire (808) – Hull	AEC	part of vintage vehicle fleet
191	AST416A	London Bus Services Ltd	AEC	in storage
192	NMB576	Novia Livsmedelsindustries, Kristianstrad, Sweden	AEC	
194	60 6625	Gampala Bus Company Ltd, Sri Lanka – Negombo depot (NB109)	AEC	
196	VLT196	Mr D. Brown, Muswell Hill	AEC	preserved
200	VLT200	Messrs W Brydon & K Perrett, Cowdenbeath	AEC	preserved
202	VLT202	London Central – New Cross	Scania	
204	LDS233A	Hontakasagoya Co Ltd, Kobe, Japan	AEC	use unknown
206	ESH286	Thermote & Vanhalst, Gullegem, Belgium	AEC	hospitality vehicle
209	ANV820	Mr P. Dejans, Deinze, Belgium	AEC	open top conversion 1986, promotional vehicle
216	VLT216	GEC Marconi Dynamics Ltd, Stanmore	AEC	Project vehicle
219	WXA200T	Hator, Warsaw, Poland	AEC	promotional vehicle, Clydemaster refurbishment in 1989
221	SD4295	Wanaka Lucern Ltd., Wanaka, South Island, New Zealand	AEC	open top
223	AX54643	Mr K. Naheed, Lillestrom, Norway	AEC	out of use
226	3563-RL-13	M L. Turcat, Martigues (13), France	AEC	restaurant
229	YVS294	Brakell Omnibus Sales, Cheam	AEC	for re-sale
232	U232	Stormyri, Ritell, Bjugn, near Trondheim, Norway	AEC	preserved
234	PRF573	Mr K. Heirman et al, Lede, near Aalst, Belgium	AEC	open top
235	VLT235	Arriva Presenting London – Wandsworth	AEC	rebuilt & reclassified ERM in 1990
237	VLT237	Arriva Presenting London – Wandsworth	AEC	rebuilt & reclassified ERM in 1990
238	VLT238	Fuzzy Duzzy Children's Entertainer, Abbots Langley	AEC	open top
242	VLT242	Arriva Presenting London – Wandsworth	AEC	rebuilt & reclassified ERM in 1990
244	XVS839	Mr D. Hawkins, Bridgend, Wales	AEC	
245	LDS282A	Renault Agriculture, Shipston-on-Stour	AEC	promotional vehicle
254	VLT254	Mr G. Rixon, East Molesey	AEC	preserved
255	HVS935	Green Bohemia Ltd., Hertford	AEC	promotional vehicle
259	VLT259	International Coachlines, Thornton Heath	AEC	platform doors fitted in 1996
264	??	Unknown owner, Milan, Italy	AEC	Re-registered prior to sale from UK
268	VLT268	Metroline – Holloway	AEC	
272	LDS236A	The Big Bus Co, London	AEC	blind boxes panelled over, numbered as RM 236
275	VLT275	Arriva London South – Brixton	Iveco	

RM	Registration	Present owner	Engine	Notes
281	VLT281	Arriva Presenting London – Wandsworth	AEC	rebuilt & reclassified ERM in 1990
283	60 6623	Negombo Peopolised Transport Services, Negombo, Sri Lanka	AEC	
286	VLT286	Discount Shop 31, Chiba, Tokyo, Japan	AEC	use unknown
291	VLT291	Mr K. McGowan, Rotherhithe	AEC	preserved
295	VLT295	Arriva London South – Brixton	Cummins	refurbished in 2000
298	WTS245A	Blue Triangle, Rainham, Essex	AEC	in storage
305	LDS256A	Mr P. Dejans, Deinze, Belgium	AEC	unused since acquired
307	WLT307	Arriva Presenting London – Wandsworth	AEC	open top and wheelchair lift fitted 1988
308	WLT308	Mr K. Saunders, London	AEC	preserved
311	KGJ142A	Arriva London – South Brixton	Iveco	refurbished in 1997
312	WLT312	Exported to Tokyo, Japan	AEC	use unknown
313	WSJ739	Arriva London North – Enfield	AEC	convertible open top and doors fitted in 1991, withdrawn
316	WLT316	Mr D. Hawkins, Bridgend, Wales	AEC	
317	WLT317	Ushuaia City Tour, Ushuaia, Patagonia, Argentina	AEC	for sightseeing tour
318	WLT318	Mr R Barnham, Surrey, British Columbia, Canada	AEC	static advert for 'United Used Auto & Truck Parts', for sale
321	YTS824A	Mr J. Holly, Zakopane, Poland	AEC	promotional vehicle
324	WLT324	London Bus Services Ltd	AEC	in storage
326	WLT326	A C Brain Co. (3), Osaka, Japan	Leyland	offside emergency exits fitted, promotional vehicle
327	60 6635	Gampala Bus Company Ltd, Sri Lanka – Negombo depot	Ashok	
329	MFF578	Mr J. Miller, Enfield	AEC	preserved, for sale
333	60 6612	Colombo Metropolitan Bus Company Ltd, Sri Lanka - Ratmanlana depot (RL7)	AEC	
335	WLT335	T P S Technitube Rohrenwerke Gmbh, Duan, Germany	AEC	
339	MFF582	Mrs C. Vannier, Toulouse, France	AEC	promotional vehicle, open top,
342	KFF277	Moscow South Novopodmos, Moscow, Russia	AEC	
344	60 6636	Sri Lanka Central Transport Board, Sri Lanka	AEC	(no recent report of this vehicle)
346	SVS615	Unknown owner, Milan, Italy	Iveco	promotional vehicle
348	WLT348	Arriva London South – Brixton	Iveco	
349	WLT349	Mr D. Good, Croydon	AEC	preserved
354	MHN438	Star & Liten AB, Stockholm, Sweden	AEC	
357	YVS288	Nostalgiabus, Mitcham	AEC	under conversion to open top
359	6286-RX-59	Sollac Steel Works, Dunkirk (59), France	AEC	named Jerry
364	RWC2525	Van Pur Brewery, Rzeszów, Poland	AEC	promotional vehicle
371	WLT371	Mac Tours, Cockenzie	AEC	under conversion to open top
376	WLT376	J W E Banks Ltd, Crowland	AEC	
385	WLT385	Arriva London South – Brixton	Iveco	
388	EDS300A	Yorkshire Belles, Haxby	AEC	rebuilt with open staircase in 1994, out of use
395	DECKSR3	L A Motor Coach Co, Marina del Rey, near Los Angeles, California, USA	Iveco	open top
398	WKA999W	Hator, Warsaw, Poland	AEC	open top plus doors, promotional vehicle
406	WLT406	Dualway Coaches, Rathcoole, Ireland	AEC	
408	KVS599	Mr A. Boath, Norwood Green	AEC	'Auntie Katie' – converted to open top in 1996
413	WLT413	Mr Sisi, Carai SRL, Citta Di Castelo, Italy	AEC	
416	LDS237A	McDonalds Restaurant, Rum, near Innsbruck, Austria	AEC	static childrens' Party Bus
421	WLT421	Mr E. Tapanines, Kuopio, Finland	Leyland	
428	WLT428	Imperial Buses, Rainham, Essex	AEC	open top conversion in 1986, in storage
429	XMD81A	Mr A. Boath, Norwood Green	AEC	
432	SVS617	Arriva London – South Brixton	Iveco	
435	60 6620	Colombo Metropolitan Bus Company Ltd, Sri Lanka – Maharagama depot	AEC	
436	WLT436	London Central – New Cross	Scania	refurbished in 2000
438	PO 17825	London Transport Advertising, Poznán, Poland	AEC	open top conversion in 1986
441	LDS341A	London Bus Services Ltd	AEC	in storage

RM	Registration	Present owner	Engine	Notes
444	LDS150A	Mr R. Jakob, Schweinfurt, Germany	AEC	
446	WLT446	Metroline Holloway	AEC	
447	YVS293	Lord Palumbo, Plano, Chicago, Illinois, USA	AEC	
450	WLT450	North Kent Express – Northfleet	AEC	open top plus centre entrance fitted in 1988
457	WLT457	Faud Nassif, Bekkaa Valley, Lebanon	AEC	
459	7920-WJ-14	Mr E. Huet, Hotel Climat de France, Pont L'Eveque (14), France	AEC	
460	WLT460	London Bus Export, Chepstow	AEC	
467	XVS851	Arriva London South – Brixton	Iveco	
470	D HF 1H	H Hertfurtner, Dusseldorf, Germany	Iveco	open top, Transmatic lighting fitted to lower deck in 1988
471	KVS601	International Coachlines, Thornton Heath	AEC	platform doors fitted in 1997
478	WLT478	London Central – New Cross	Scania	refurbished in 2000
479	WSJ737	Timebus Travel, St Albans	AEC	convertible open top plus doors fitted by London Coaches in 1991
494	JLL030	Twins, Antwerp, Belgium	Leyland	open top, promotional vehicle
496	WLT496	Kariuizawa Classic Car Museum, Nagano, Japan	Leyland	at Matsuda Collection, Matsuda
498	ECW313	Båstad Buss Co., Båstad, Sweden	AEC	
499	60 2542	Colombo Metropolitan Bus Company Ltd., Sri Lanka - Ratmanlana depot (RL11)	Leyland	
504	BJ2 490	1000 Islands Gananoque Chamber of Commerce, Gananoque, Ontario Canada	AEC	open top
506	WLT506	West Midlands Vintage Vehicle Society, Birmingham	Leyland	preserved
512	2NMC80	Senor I. Vargas, Cancun, Mexico	AEC	'Tuesday' – courtesy bus for La Boom night club
516	KAG884C	Homegrown, Nairobi, Kenya (T10)	AEC	staff transport
521	WLT521	Mars Confectionery, Riyadh, Saudi Arabia	AEC	promotional vehicle
525	WLT525	Unknown owner, USA	AEC	location and use unknown
527	JSJ752	Unknown owner, Czech Republic	AEC	location and use unknown
529	WLT529	Mr M. Dare, Caversham	AEC	preserved
531	WLT531	Arriva London South – Brixton	Scania	refurbished in 2000
541	WLT541	London Central – New Cross	Scania	
545	WLT545	Arriva Presenting London – Wandsworth	DAF	
546	LDS284A	Autohaus Schnolzer Gmbh, Gelzenkirchen, Germany	AEC	Transmatic lighting fitted in 1991
548	SVS618	Marie Cuire Cancer Project	Iveco	location unknown
549	AA29300	Halden Trafikk, Halden, Norway	Leyland	
550	LDS184A	Mr H Grimm, Play & Fun Gmbh, Plauen, Germany	AEC	door fitted to platform, last reported at Ohrdruf
552	1823VE80	Association ABA, Amiens (80), France	AEC	
555	WLT555	unknown owner, Germany	AEC	open top, location and use unknown
560	EDS50A	Bluebird Buses (1102) – Lathalmond	AEC	A1 Service livery
564	WLT564	Unknown owner, Tokyo, Japan	Leyland	last reported at Midosiyi Boulevard as a wine bar
577	WLT577	Mr R. Zarywacz, Reading	AEC	preserved
581	WLT581	Stephen Austin Newspapers, Hertford	AEC	open top conversion in 1985
583	BJ2 736	Double Deck Tours (5), Niagara Falls, Ontario, Canada	AEC	fitted with platform door in 1999
584	WLT584	Karinord Oy, Kauhava, Finland	AEC	use unknown, numbered as RM 943
592	WLT592	Unknown owner, Japan	AEC	location and use unknown
596	60 6632	Gampala Bus Company Ltd, Sri Lanka – Negombo depot (NB108)	AEC	
597	WLT597	Mr K. Currall, Longford	AEC	preserved
598	DECKSR2	L A Motor Coach Co, Marina del Rey, Near Los Angeles, California, USA	Iveco	open top
599	T23 880	Daisy Tours, San Antonio, Texas, USA	Iveco	right hand sliding entrance door
600	WLT600	Mr Matsugi, Matsuyama-City, Ehime, Japan	AEC	use unknown

RM	Registration	Present owner	Engine	Notes
606	EDS320A	Unknown owner, Glasgow	AEC	preserved, re-reg, fluorescent lighting fitted in 1991
611	6295-RX-59	Sollac Steel Works, Nantes, France	AEC	named Jerry
613	WLT613	Stagecoach East London – Upton Park	AEC	
621	WLT621	Unknown owner, Argentina	AEC	location and use unknown
625	PLR725	Aspekt Mobiel, Zandhoven, Belgium	AEC	open top
626	NEL88	London Bus Transport Oy, Espoo, Finland	Leyland	last recorded operating in Helsinki,
632	WLT632	McDonalds Restaurants, Tokyo, Japan	AEC	Party bus
638	WLT638	Mitsui Greenland, Kumamoto, Japan	AEC	static at Kumakoto Theme Park
641	WLT641	Mr Eistel, Menden, Germany	AEC	Hospitality vehicle
642	WLT642	Mr P. Simmonds, Morden	AEC	preserved
644	WLT644	Metroline – Willesden	AEC	open top conversion 1988, doors fitted 1993
646	KFF257	Metroline – Holloway	AEC	
648	XVS826	exported to unknown owner	AEC	location and use unknown
649	60 6642	Ruhunu Bus Company Ltd, Sri Lanka – Galle depot (GL72)	AEC	
652	WLT652	Mr G. Watson, Chesterfield	AEC	preserved, fitted with Transmatic lighting in 1993, named 'Rodney the Routemaster'
654	WLT654	Messrs M. Begley & D. Cartmill, Belfast, Northern Ireland	AEC	preserved, Leyland engine
655	WLT655	Confidence Bus & Coach Hire(15), Oadby	Leyland	
659	KFF239	London Bus Services Ltd	AEC	in storage
663	A11 963	Unknown owner, The Geispe Peninsula, Quebec, Canada	AEC	door fitted to platform, reported as undergoing conversion into a restaurant
664	WLT664	Arriva London South – Brixton	Iveco	
666	WLT875	Messrs K Bevan, P Denham, C Sparkes, Newport, Gwent	AEC	preserved, renumbered RM 875 in 1994
676	WLT676	Arriva London South – Brixton	Iveco	
682	HVS937	Mr J.B. Wowor, Ridderkerk, Netherlands	AEC	
687	WLT687	London Central – New Cross	Scania	
696	XVS829	Garage SR PL, nr. Toulouse (31), France	AEC	
697	LDS238A	Mr A. Beattie, London	AEC	Fish and Chip bar in Barking
698	WLT698	Parque de la Costa, Tigre, Buenos Aires, Argentina	AEC	
699	PAN696	Mr S. Bjork, Ljunskile, Sweden	AEC	
702	WTS404A	Garage 'Ideal Auto', Soual (81), France	AEC	
706	PO 06014	London Transport Advertising, Poznán, Poland	AEC	
709	DD JL 63	Hans Grd, Vastert, Germany	AEC	Mobile restaurant
710	WLT710	PVS, Barnsley	—	for re-sale
713	TSK270	Unknown owner, Italy	AEC	location and use unknown
715	WLT715	Unknown owner, Tokyo, Japan	AEC	use unknown
718	BS-04-96	Roda British Transport & Promotions, Arnhem, The Netherlands	AEC	
719	WLT719	Arriva London South – Brixton	Iveco	
720	ZH-332-71U	Londag, Basserdorf, Switzerland	AEC	exhibition unit for Apple Computers, fitted with canvas roof
727	LDS239A	East Yorkshire (817) – Scarborough	AEC	refurbished by SYT in 1993, converted to open-top in 1999
730	60 6624	Gampala Bus Company Ltd., Sri Lanka – Negombo depot	AEC	
731	60 6640	Mahanuwara Bus Company Ltd., Sri Lanka – Yatinuwara depot (YT101)	AEC	all over advert livery for Mitsui cement
732	NRH801A	McDonalds Restaurants, Modena, Italy	AEC	refurbished by SYT in 1993
735	1NLC87	Senor I. Vargas, Cancun, Mexico	AEC	'Monday' – courtesy bus for La Boom night club, open top
736	XYJ418	Arriva London South – Brixton	Cummins	refurbished in 2000

RM	Registration	Present owner	Engine	Notes
737	WLT737	RM 737 Group, Harrow	AEC	preserved
742	WLT742	Mr D. Eastell, Louth	AEC	part open top conversion in 1987, t/a Red Bus Jolly Jaunts
746	60 6611	Colombo South Region Transport Board, Sri Lanka – Maharagama depot	AEC	(no recent report of this vehicle)
751	KGH889A	HafneruFliesenlegergewerbe, Wilhelmsberg, Austria	AEC	bodywork lowered to 4 metres in height
752	WLT752	Arriva Presenting London – Wandsworth	AEC	open top conversion in 1986, BTA overall advert
753	WLT753	Arriva Presenting London – Wandsworth	AEC	open top conversion in 1988
757	NVS855	Lakeland Hotel, Monnickendam, The Netherlands	AEC	
758	WLT758	London Central – New Cross	Scania	
759	WLT759	Mr M. Roulston, Glasgow	AEC	preserved in Glasgow Corporation style livery
765	WLT765	Messrs I. Townsend, T. Marshall & E Miller, Nottingham	AEC	Preserved
769	WLT769	Zadian SRL, Neroto Teramo, Italy	AEC	
775	WLT775	Ringsted Energy Centre, Ringsted, Denmark	AEC	
781	62??-RX-59	Sollac Steel Works, Dunkirk, France	AEC	named 'Tom'
782	WLT782	London Central – New Cross	Scania	
785	WLT785	Nijinsato Theme Park, Shuzenji, Shizuoka, Japan	AEC	Restaurant with air conditioning
787	WLT787	London Central – New Cross	Scania	
788	WLT788	Unknown owner, Hungary	AEC	roadside café between Kiskunfelegyhaza and Kistelek
790	WLT790	Unknown owner, Argentina	AEC	location and use unknown
794	BF7 312	AA99 Inc, t/a Holiday VIP Tours, Niagara Falls, Canada	AEC	covered in old pennies and a 'Big Ben', withdrawn
795	WLT795	AJ & NM Carr Ltd., Pluckley	AEC	former promotional/hospitality vehicle, in storage after use as 'The Nose Bus' in 1999
797	BA4 845	Double Deck Tours (17), Niagara Falls, Ontario, Canada	AEC	
798	NRH802A	Prirodni Svet, Usti nad Labem, Czech Republic	AEC	preserved
799	EDS312A	exported to unknown owner	AEC	location and use unknown
800	60 6628	Negombo Peopolised Transport Services, Negombo, Sri Lanka	AEC	
804	CJS112	Seagram United Kingdom Ltd, London	AEC	numbered as RM214, awaiting export to Belgrade, Yugoslavia
809	HWU935	Routemaster Travel, Vaxjo, Sweden	AEC	
811	WLT811	David Shepherd Conservation Foundation – Preston	AEC	promotional vehicle
812	LFK381	Mr P. Roisin, Bus Prophils, Chatelet, Belgium	AEC	part open top
820	WLT820	Sakurai Ham, Kanagawa, Japan	Leyland	open top
822	WLT822	Mr G. Sibbons, Billericay	AEC	preserved
824	PO 06015	London Transport Advertising, Poznán, Poland	AEC	
826	KFF252	Marku Immden, Tamtere, Finland	AEC	use unknown
828	WLT828	Halden Trafikk, Halden, Norway	Leyland	out of use
831	—	Auto Recoveries, Carlisle	—	turnover vehicle
832	BHU987A	Unknown owner, Germany	AEC	location and use unknown
835	WLT835	Clydemaster Preservation Group, Brentwood	AEC	preserved
837	KGJ62A	exported to unknown owner	AEC	location and use unknown
838	XYJ440	London Bus Services Ltd	AEC	in storage
843	XVS828	Unknown owner, Sussex	AEC	promotional vehicle
848	WLT848	London Bus Services Ltd	—	in storage
851	WLT851	Bus It, Tokyo, Japan	AEC	Mens Boutique
852	60 6610	Colombo Metropolitan Bus Company Ltd, Sri Lanka – Maharagama depot (RL8)	AEC	
857	WLT857	Unknown owner, London	Leyland	mobile home
859	LFK381	Ceremonie Roger, Meulebeke, Belgium	AEC	
868	NSJ940	Seger Europe AB, Galstad, Sweden	AEC	promotional vehicle

RM	Registration	Present owner	Engine	Notes
871	WLT871	London Bus Services Ltd	AEC	in storage
872	JSJ767	F.S.Distribution, Thame, Oxon	AEC	promotional vehicle, used by BBC
875	OVS940	London Bus Services Ltd	AEC	in storage
879	WLT879	Hator, Warsaw, Poland	Leyland	
905	16E8077	Fruk-Tamek Meyan Sulari, Sanayii AS, Istanbul, Turkey	AEC	promotional vehicle for Pepsi Cola,
909	WTS418A	Mr B. Walker, Eastham, Wirral	AEC	preserved in Western livery
910	EDS288A	Mr R. Thomas, c/o Edinburgh Transport Group, Glasgow	AEC	preserved in Edinburgh Corporation livery
912	WLT912	Mr R. Sullivan, Shanklin, Isle of Wight	AEC	preserved
918	NNY023	Mr O. Haack, Gotland, Sweden	AEC	in use in Visby, rebuilt with offside exit
924	LDS260A	McDonalds Restaurants, Heerlen, Spekholzerheide, The Netherlands	AEC	static children's party bus
928	WLT928	London Central – New Cross	Scania	
931	MFF580	London Bus Services Ltd	AEC	in storage
933	WLT933	exported to unknown owner	AEC	Transmatic lighting fitted by Western in 1989, location and use unknown
937	WLT937	Absolute Charter Inc, Halifax, Nova Scotia, Canada	AEC	Transmatic lighting fitted by Southend Transport in 1988
938	WLT938	Mr I. Hoskin, Mitcham	AEC	preserved, Reading Mainline (100)
943	WSY333	Unknown owner, Japan	AEC	Children's waiting room
944	JDU536	Music Hall Theatre Co, Brussels, Belgium	AEC	used as a mobile theatre, open top conversion in 1995
946	MFF577	Senor I. Vargas, Cancun, Mexico	AEC	'Friday' – courtesy bus for La Boom night club
949	WXA010W	Hator, Warsaw, Poland	AEC	Transmatic lighting fitted by Southend Transport in 1988
951	U59 133	Mr J. Moore, Hillsboro, Texas, USA	AEC	preserved
956	LDS261A	Mr R. di Corso, La Cibab SRL, Sarzana, Italy	AEC	lower deck converted to an English style pub
960	WLT960	Mr A. Gregory, Croydon	AEC	preserved
963	399 BWJ	Ms J. Foley, Snohomish, Washington, USA	AEC	preserved
966	LSL827	Nacro, Brighton, Sussex	AEC	mobile IT classroom
967	WLT967	London Central – New Cross	Scania	
969	DFH806A	Unknown owner, Argentina	Leyland	location and use unknown
970	WLT970	Arriva London South – Brixton	Iveco	
977	ENN604	Maison Communale Des Jeunes, Huy, Belgium	AEC	For use by a youth club
978	LDS164A	Messrs A. Harlott & A Brown, Romford	AEC	undergoing conversion to open top
980	USK625	Stagecoach East London – Upton Park	Scania	refurbished by East London in 1997
982	NVS804	De Souza, Buenos Aires, Argentina	AEC	open top, courtesy vehicle
986	BE9 683	Capital Double Decker & Trolley Tours, Ottawa, Canada	Leyland	out of use, for spares
991	WLT991	Mr E. Dickenson, Timperley	AEC	preserved
994	WLT994	London General – Waterloo	Iveco	refurbished by Northern Counties in 1992
995	WLT995	Mr V. Zolak, Budva, Montenegro, Yugoslavia	AEC	for conversion to a café
997	WLT997	Arriva London South – Brixton	Iveco	
999	WVS423	Reading Heritage Travel	AEC	
1000	100BXL	RM1000 Group, Croydon	AEC	preserved
1001	1CLT	Mr M. Smith, Billericay	AEC	preserved
1002	OYM368A	London Central – New Cross	Scania	
1003	3CLT	Arriva London South – Brixton	Iveco	
1005	ALC290A	London Bus Services Ltd	AEC	in storage
1006	FZV328	Publi-bus, Meeuwen-Gruitrode, Belgium	AEC	platform doors fitted
1009	9CLT	Blue Triangle, Rainham, Essex	AEC	in storage
1010	EDS221A	East Yorkshire (819) – Scarborough	AEC	open top conversion in 1996
1013	LDS253A	Mr A. Soucek, Prague, Czech Republic	AEC	
1017	YTS973A	Unknown owner, Argentina	AEC	location and use unknown
1018	PVS828	London Bus Services Ltd.	AEC	in storage
1020	PVS830	Abaco Vox d.o.o., Zagreb, Croatia	AEC	promotional vehicle
1026	26CLT	Unknown owner, Spain	Leyland	location and use unknown
1029	60 6626	Gampala Bus Company Ltd., Sri Lanka – Negombo depot	AEC	

RM	Registration	Present owner	Engine	Notes
1033	DSL540	London Central – New Cross	Scania	refurbished in 2000
1041	NRH805A	Herve SARL, Vannes (56), France	AEC	
1047	47CLT	Mr O. Vorlander, Ruppichferath, Germany	AEC	
1053	YVS287	Hator, Warsaw, Poland	AEC	
1054	LDS285A	Rheinheimer Autoteile, Krickenbach, Germany	AEC	re-reg LDS285A by Western in 1990
1058	58CLT	London Central – New Cross	Scania	refurbished in 2000
1061	BE9503	New York Shafa Tours, New York, USA	AEC	open top
1062	62CLT	London Central – New Cross	Scania	
1063	63CLT	Mr D. Ladd, Richings Park	AEC	preserved
1067	60 6633	Negombo Peopolised Transport Services, Negombo, Sri Lanka	AEC	
1068	2NMC82	Senor I. Vargas, Cancun, Mexico	AEC	'Wednesday' – courtesy bus for La Boom night club
1069	69CLT	Sullivan Buses, Potters Bar	AEC	
1070	SLZ970	Parque de la Costa, Tigre, Buenos Aires, Argentina	AEC	
1072	HVS983	Duke of Kent Bus Tours, Mississauga, Ontario, Canada	AEC	
1077	KGH26A	Handelsbolaget Rode Orm, Mariehamm, Aland Is, Finland	AEC	operates a tourist service
1078	KGH925A	LA Motor Coach Co, Marina del Rey, near Los Angeles, California, USA	AEC	
1080	60 6621	Colombo Metropolitan Bus Company Ltd, Sri Lanka – Maharagama depot (RL6)	AEC	
1082	82CLT	London Central – New Cross	Scania	refurbished in 2000
1083	XVS850	International Coachlines, Thornton Heath	Iveco	platform doors fitted in 1995
1086	86CLT	Mr Kristensen, Ans, Denmark	AEC	located in his scrap yard
1087	87CLT	Mr E. Riccombeni, Miami, Florida, USA	AEC	for sale, open top
1088	88CLT	McDonalds Restaurants, La Louviere, Belgium	AEC	static childrens' party bus
1090	90CLT	A C Brain Co, Osaka, Japan	AEC	offside emergency exits fitted, promotional vehicle, numbered as RM 326
1097	97CLT	London Central – New Cross	Scania	
1101	KFF367	Friends of Wirral Transport Museum, Birkenhead	Iveco	occasional psv use in connection with Birkenhead Tramway Museum
1102	BK2 733	Double Deck Tours (19), Niagara Falls, Ontario, Canada	AEC	
1104	104CLT	London Central – New Cross	Scania	refurbished in 2000
1109	EAD314A	Unknown owner, Italy	AEC	location and use unknown
1111	111CLT	Travellers Young Fashion, Augsburg, Germany	AEC	mobile clothes shop
1115	60 6609	Colombo Metropolitan Bus Company Ltd., Sri Lanka – Ratmanlana depot (RL13)	AEC	
1117	117CLT	Unknown owner, Spain	Leyland	location and use unknown
1119	119CLT	London Central – New Cross	Scania	
1121	60 6622	Mr U. Perera, Tharanganee Garments, Peliyagoda, Sri Lanka	Isuzu	restoration project
1123	123CLT	Mr S. Nicholls, Liverpool	AEC	former promotional vehicle
1124	VYJ806	Arriva London South – Brixton	Iveco	
1125	KGH858A	Arriva London North – Clapton	Iveco	refurbished by Leaside in 1997
1131	131CLT	Kumamoto Theme Park, Kyushu, Japan	AEC	static exhibit at Asia Park
1133	KFF240	Unknown owner, France	AEC	location and use unknown
1134	YVS285	Unknown owner, Baghdad, Iraq	AEC	use unknown
1136	AOI330	Parque de la Costa, Tigre, Buenos Aires, Argentina	AEC	use unknown
1138	138CLT	Mr S. Miles, Benfleet	AEC	preserved
1145	LDS402A	Wealden PSV, Five Oak Green, Tonbridge	AEC	former film location vehicle for re-sale
1149	YVS290	Lakeland Hotel, Monnickendam, The Netherlands	AEC	
1150	60 6619	Colombo Metropolitan Bus Company Ltd, Sri Lanka – Maharagama depot (MH157)	AEC	
1152	152CLT	Mr J. Pryer, Sandbach	AEC	preserved
1154	154CLT	Nichioh Trade Services, Kobe, Japan	AEC	location and use unknown
1156	156CLT	Unknown owner, Netherlands	AEC	location and use unknown

RM	Registration	Present owner	Engine	Notes
1157	157CLT	Sopexci, Benin, West Africa	AEC	static promotional vehicle
1158	158CLT	Hamilton Square, New Jersey, USA	AEC	Reported as rebuilt with staircase and platform reversed in 1998
1159	159CLT	Mr N. Goodman, Herne Bay	Leyland	Mobile fish restaurant, open top,
1160	60 6631	Negombo Peopolised Transport Services, Sri Lanka	AEC	
1163	163CLT	Fitland Mill bv, Mill, The Netherlands	Leyland	for static advertising
1164	NSG636A	PVS, Barnsley	—	
1165	60 6641	Sri Lanka Central Transport Board	AEC	(no recent report of this vehicle)
1166	GVS498	Sr R. Tornabell, Sta. Eulalia D'Roachz, Barcelona, Spain	AEC	for use by an advertising agency
1168	168CLT	London Central – New Cross	Scania	refurbished in 2000
1170	KAG004C	Homegrown, Nairobi, Kenya (T6)	AEC	staff transport
1171	171CLT	exported to unknown owner	AEC	location and use unknown
1174	JSJ797	London Central – New Cross	Scania	
1176	??	Unknown owner, Czech Republic	AEC	location and use unknown
1180	B1180	Routemaster ASBL, Luxembourg	AEC	preserved
1181	KN-C-989	Mr P. Brandes, Konstanz, Germany	AEC	publicity vehicle for the musical 'Cats', bodywork lowered to under 13 foot,
1185	XYJ427	Unknown owner, Waterloo	AEC	for conversion to a coffee/tea-bar
1187	2454	Nagasaki Kenie Bus Co, Nagasaki, Japan	AEC	open-top with doors fitted, used on sightseeing tours
1192	192CLT	Unknown owner, Fukuoka City, Japan	AEC	in use as a bar, doors fitted to platform
1197	KGJ29A	Café de la CroixBlanche, Posieux, Switzerland	AEC	static coffee shop
1204	204CLT	London Bus Services Ltd	AEC	in storage
1205	XYJ429	Unknown owner, Spain	AEC	location and use unknown
1212	212CLT	Harbarth & Shenton, Lipperbruch, Germany	AEC	
1214	214CLT	Halifax Joint Committee (39)	AEC	
1218	218CLT	London Bus Services Ltd	AEC	in storage
1221	HVR203	Mr P. Pesikaka, Tottenham, Ontario, Canada (9)	AEC	t/a London Picadilly Buses
1224	UYJ654	Mr W. Liddle, Colindale	AEC	preserved
1242	BC8 553	Double Deck Tours (8), Niagara Falls, Ontario, Canada	Leyland	
1243	60 6630	Gampala Bus Company Ltd., Sri Lanka – Negombo depot	AEC	
1245	LDS210A	London Bus Services Ltd	AEC	in storage
1248	248CLT	Kariuizawa Classic Car Museum, Nagano, Japan	–	engine removed prior to export
1251	251CLT	Mr S. Sano, Takamatsu-City, Japan	AEC	use unknown
1257	KAG154C	Homegrown, Nairobi, Kenya (T8)	AEC	staff transport
1260	JSJ743	London Central – New Cross	Scania	
1262	VYJ876	PVS, Barnsley	AEC	playbus, for re-sale
1266	266CLT	Unknown owner, Argentina	AEC	location and use unknown
1271	29-67-MA	Cabriolet Cars, Funchal, Madeira, Portugal	AEC	central offside door fitted and platform panelled over, open-top, out of use
1274	LDS67A	The Crescent Project, Bisley	AEC	mobile youth club, 'The Web Bus'
1280	280CLT	London Bus Services Ltd	AEC	in storage
1282	16E8076	Fruk-Tamek Meyan Sulari, Sanayii AS, Istanbul, Turkey	AEC	promotional vehicle for Yedigan Light (soft drink)
1283	283CLT	exported to unknown owner	AEC	location and use unknown
1288	HK1931	Citybus, Kowloon, Hong Kong (1)	Leyland	rebuilt to vintage open top style
1289	XSL596A	Stagecoach East London – Upton Park	Scania	refurbished by East London in 1997
1292	NVS485	Mr T. Peters, London	AEC	
1294	60 6637	Negombo Peopolised Transport Services, Negombo, Sri Lanka	AEC	
1305	305CLT	London Central – New Cross	Scania	
1312	MFF509	London Bus Services Ltd	Leyland	in storage
1313	M89772	Mr J. Doe, c/o Holiday Inn, Quincy, Illinois, USA	AEC	
1314	314CLT	Sonesta Hotel, Sonesta Beach Resort, Bermuda	AEC	
1316	316CLT	F C Muntaner Mataix, Alicante, Spain	AEC	

RM	Registration	Present owner	Engine	Notes
1321	321CLT	Mr B. Walker, Eastham, Wirral	AEC	preserved
1324	324CLT	Arriva London South – Brixton	Iveco	refurbished in 2000
1330	KGH975A	Arriva London South – Brixton	Cummins	refurbished in 2000
1336	60 6608	Colombo Metropolitan Bus Company Ltd., Sri Lanka – Maharagama depot (MH153)	AEC	
1339	339CLT	Yamada Real Estate Agency, Osaka, Japan	AEC	Restaurant
1348	348CLT	Metroline – Holloway	AEC	
1353	353CLT	Mr J. Coombes, Groes Faen, nr. Cardiff	AEC	preserved
1357	357CLT	Unknown owner	Leyland	for conversion internally into a submarine
1359	359CLT	Riparo Auto SNC, Palermo, Sicily, Italy	AEC	
1361	VYJ808	Arriva London South – Brixton	Iveco	
1363	363CLT	Mr C Knight, Badminton	Leyland	preserved
1364	60 6606	Ruhunu Bus Company Ltd., Sri Lanka – Galle depot (GL71)	AEC	
1366	NKH807A	SMN Aussenhandels, Sophia, Bulgaria	AEC	
1368	368CLT	Mr A. Morgan, St Albans	AEC	converted to single-deck by LT in 1975, preserved
1371	PVA046	Abegweit Sightseeing Tours, Charlottetown, Prince Edward Island, Canada	Leyland	
1380	380CLT	London Central – New Cross	Scania	refurbished in 2000
1384	384CLT	Tea & Pub 'Double Decker', Tokyo, Japan	AEC	tea and pub house
1394	394CLT	Nostalgiabus, Mitcham	AEC	
1397	71AWN	Mr A. Naish, Loughborough	Leyland	preserved
1398	KGJ118A	Arriva London South – Brixton	Iveco	
1400	KGJ339A	London Central – New Cross	Scania	
1401	60 6639	North Western Region Transport Board, Sri Lanka – Wennappuwu (WP53)	AEC	
1403	403CLT	Mr P. & D. Sapte et al, Watford	Leyland	preserved, open top conversion by LT in 1984
1404	404CLT	Koyama Driving School, Kanagawa, Japan	Leyland	waiting room
1413	60 6629	Gampala Bus Company Ltd., Sri Lanka – Negombo depot	AEC	
1414	414CLT	Museum of Transport, Manchester	Leyland	vehicle donated by LTE
1415	AP.6119	Unknown owner, last reported at Ste Eustache, Quebec, Canada	AEC	platform doors fitted, location and use unknown, numbered as RM 663
1417	417CLT	Artas Promotions, Budapest, Hungary	Leyland	
1421	AEW440A	exported to unknown owner	AEC	location and use unknown
1424	BC9 998	Mr M. Hollander, North Gower, Ontario, Canada	–	out of use, engine removed
1425	3195WF42	Mr B. Henrion, St Etienne (42), France	AEC	static snack bar at the Trefilerie University
1428	428CLT	Unknown owner, Belgium	AEC	location and use unknown
1433	433CLT	Mr B. Maniglia, Minerbio, Italy	AEC	Personnel and Motorcycle transporter, roof lowered and partially open-top
1448	—	Mr T. Mulligan, Stittsville, Ontario, Canada	—	registered BC9 997 (but not carried), Burger and ice cream bar, engineless
1449	449CLT	Mr R. Kemp, Battersea	AEC	occasional psv use with Liverpool Motor Services
1522	522CLT	Unknown owner, Portoroz, Slovenia	Leyland	condition unknown
1526	526CLT	Unknown owner, Spain	Leyland	location and use unknown
1527	527CLT	Stagecoach East London – Upton Park	AEC	frequently loaned to BBCtv at Elstree for Eastenders TV series
1528	KGJ117A	Tourex, Oxford	Iveco	being prepared for future use
1530	60 6607	Colombo Metropolitan Bus Company Ltd., Sri Lanka – Maharagama depot	AEC	
1531	531CLT	Unknown owner, Spain	AEC	location and use unknown
1539	539CLT	Unknown owner, Japan	Leyland	last reported in use as a restaurant, location and use unknown
1543	543CLT	Mr P. Watson, Cheam	Leyland	preserved
1545	KGJ37A	Exported to Paraguay	AEC	location and use unknown
1546	546CLT	Unknown owner, Japan	Leyland	location and use unknown
1548	BC8 554	Double Deck Tours (11), Niagara Falls, Ontario, Canada	Leyland	
1549	549CLT	Zakkaya, Saitama, Japan	Leyland	used as a grocery shop, fitted with platform doors
1555	EBY315B	Domino Steak House, Eupen, Belgium	AEC	
1562	562CLT	Friends of the LT Museum	AEC	At Acton 'Depot'

RM	Registration	Present owner	Engine	Notes
1563	563CLT	Mr N. Townsend, Chiswick	Leyland	preserved
1568	BNK324A	London Bus Services Ltd	AEC	in storage
1571	571CLT	Nostalgiabus, Mitcham	AEC	open top conversion 2000
1581	60 6634	Gampala Bus Company Lt., Sri Lanka – Negombo depot	AEC	
1583	583CLT	Walkabout Inns, Muswell Hill	AEC	
1585	ALC459A	London Bus SARL, Tallende (63), France	AEC	stored, not yet in use
1590	RSL259	Metro Bus Sales, Braintree, Essex	Iveco	door fitted to platform, for re-sale
1593	593CLT	Arriva London South – Brixton	Iveco	
1599	YTS820A	Stagecoach East London – Upton Park	Scania	refurbished by East London in 1997
1604	BJ6 939	Double Deck Tours (18), Niagara Falls, Ontario, Canada	AEC	
1607	LDS201A	Bluebird Buses (1107) – Lathalmond	AEC	part of Stagecoach preserved fleet
1609	609DYE	London Bus SARL, Tallende (63), France	AEC	stored, not yet in use
1611	611DYE	The City of Oxford, Oxford, Missouri, USA	AEC	open top, used on city sightseeing tours
1618	BA4 802	Double Deck Tours (10), Niagara Falls, Ontario, Canada	AEC	platform doors fitted 2000
1619	KGJ188A	Unknown owner, Japan	AEC	location and use unknown
1620	PVA079	Abegweit Sightseeing Tours, Charlottetown, Prince Edward Island, Canada	Leyland	
1621	KGJ187A	London Central – New Cross	Scania	refurbished in 2000
1627	627DYE	London Bus Services Ltd	AEC	in storage
1630	EDS537B	F R de Languana, Las Palmas, Grand Canaria, Canary Islands	AEC	reported in use with a hotel chain, open top
1640	640DYE	London Bus Services Ltd	AEC	in storage
1641	641DYE	Imperial Buses, Rainham, Essex	Leyland	in storage
1643	643DYE	Queen Elizabeth Hospital, Edgbaston	Leyland	promotional vehicle for the Renal unit
1647	BNK32A	Senor I. Vargas, Cancun, Mexico	AEC	'Thursday' – courtesy bus for La Boom night club
1649	649DYE	Sound Prop, Budapest, Hungary	Leyland	
1650	650DYE	London Bus Services Ltd	Leyland	in storage
1651	BA4 805	Double Deck Tours (3), Niagara Falls, Ontario, Canada	Leyland	fitted with RTW roof
1654	654DYE	Mr D. Forrest, Southampton	Leyland	preserved
1660	NC7416	Leisure Concepts Double Decker Bus Tours Division, Queenstown, South Island, New Zealand	Leyland	t/a Arrowtown Sightseeing
1666	KGJ341A	London Central – New Cross	Scania	
1670	4HIRE2	The Party Bus Co, Auckland, North Island, New Zealand	Hino	t/a Double Deck Bus Charters
1676	BK2 734	Double Deck Tours (22), Niagara Falls, Ontario, Canada	AEC	
1677	677DYE	Mr Francis, Chepstow	AEC	preserved
1681	681DYE	Cookagogo, Soupetard (31), near Toulouse, France	AEC	Pizza Restaurant
1682	682DYE	McDonalds Restaurants, Germany	AEC	children's party bus, location unknown
1684	684DYE	last reported as with De Dubbeldekkers, Schilde, Belgium	Leyland	location and use unknown
1691	691DYE	Mr J. Fozard, Keighley	AEC	preserved
1694	694DYE	Ciclo Tours, Spain	AEC	location and use unknown, open top
1699	699DYE	Mr S. Wood, Hertford	AEC	preserved
1700	SAN9486	Pietrucha SiA, Blaszki, Poland	AEC	promotional vehicle, platform doors fitted
1701	PAH502	Mr R. Hogber, Stockholm, Sweden	AEC	
1708	TC2323	Bus & Truck Museum, Tempe, Sydney, Australia	AEC	preserved
1711	711DYE	last reported as with De Dubbeldekkers, Schilde, Belgium	Leyland	location and use unknown
1713	713DYE	Unknown owner, Japan	Leyland	in use as a static Café at Mito station
1720	KP.109.650	Unknown owner, Portoroz, Slovenia	Leyland	condition unknown, open top
1725	725DYE	Arriva London North – Clapton	Iveco	refurbished by Leaside in 1996
1727	727DYE	exported to unknown owner	AEC	location and use unknown
1730	730DYE	A C Brain Co, Osaka, Japan	Leyland	all over advert livery
1731	HAS452	London Ceremonie Bus, Kapellen, Belgium	AEC	numbered as RM 54
1732	B4383	Mr P. Roisin, Bus Prophils, Chatelet, Belgium	Leyland	rear platform doors fitted

RM	Registration	Present owner	Engine	Notes
1734	734DYE	Arriva London South – Brixton	Iveco	
1735	735DYE	London Bus Services Ltd	AEC	in storage
1737	737DYE	London Transport Museum	AEC	on display at Covent Garden museum
1740	740DYE	94.7FM Concerto, Montevideo, Uruguay	Leyland	platform doors fitted, used during the summer time at Punte del Este
1741	WFE517S	Auto Hobby, Warsaw, Poland	Leyland	in use with Target School of English
1747	747DYE	Mr A. Boath, Norwood Green	AEC	former playbus
1752	BB4 289	Mr T. Mulligan, Stittsville, Ontario, Canada	–	engineless, out of use
1754	754DYE	Unknown owner, USA	Leyland	open top, location and use unknown
1756	U31 275	Bright Horizon Conservatoire School, Charrollton, nr Dallas, Texas, USA	Leyland	
1758	MSJ920	McDonalds Restaurant, Germany	AEC	location unknown
1767	767DYE	c/o London Bus Export Co., Chepstow	Leyland	former promotional vehicle
1771	771DYE	Warehouse Night Club, Doncaster	Leyland	
1773	BB4 292	Capital Double Deck & Trolley Tours (260), Ottawa, Ontario, Canada	Leyland	open top conversion 1995
1776	776DYE	Mr R. Brown, Haydon Bridge, Northumberland	AEC	Fish and Chip shop
1783	783DYE	Bath Bus Co., Bath	AEC	open top conversion in 1986
1788	BB4 954	Capital Double Deck & Trolley Tours (80), Ottawa, Ontario, Canada	Leyland	
1790	790DYE	London Borough of Lewisham, Catford	Leyland	door fitted to platform, playbus c/o Poverty Action Group
1791	LBB702	Mr d'Hulst et al, Lier, Belgium	Leyland	not used since acquisition
1793	793DYE	Unknown owners, Japan	Leyland	location and use unknown
1796	796DYE	Unknown owner, Himegi, Japan	AEC	'Game Corner', used as a coin-in-the-slot machine parlour on roof garden of shopping complex, platform doors fitted
1797	797DYE	London Central – New Cross	Scania	
1799	799DYE	Metroline – Willesden	AEC	
1801	801DYE	Arriva London South – Brixton	Iveco	
1804	EYY327B	Messrs M Smith, Billericay & P Watson, Cheam	AEC	preserved
1807	EVM132B	McDonalds Restaurants, Mereside, Lancashire	AEC	static children's Party Bus
1810	EBY247B	Martin Dawes Communications, Paris, France	AEC	
1811	EGF220B	Arriva London South – Brixton	Iveco	
1815	NOH.AA.100	Hi Klimmet, De Hupberg, Isterberg, Germany	AEC	publicity vehicle for Twinings Tea Makers, bodywork lowered to under 13 foot
1819	819DYE	Glenhills Co., Kagoshima, Japan	AEC	Satsuma Eikokukan restaurant
1822	822DYE	Arriva London South – Brixton	Iveco	
1825	BUR962	Municipal Council of Ypres, Belgium	AEC	
1827	60 6627	Negombo Peopolised Transport Services, Negombo, Sri Lanka	AEC	
1836	EGF285B	Mr A. Boath, Norwood Green	Leyland	open top conversion in 1995,
1840	840DYE	Mr H. Hobson, Royston	AEC	Preserved
1842	BFW544B	Mr I. Rushby, Market Rasen	AEC	mobile home
1843	843DYE	Unknown owner, USA	Leyland	location and use unknown
1851	60 6601	Colombo Metropolitan Bus Company Ltd, Sri Lanka – Maharagama depot	AEC	
1859	859DYE	Mr J. Belcher, Reading	Leyland	preserved
1864	864DYE	Arriva Presenting London – Wandsworth	Leyland	open top conversion in 1986
1871	ALD871B	Timebus Travel, St Albans	AEC	
1872	ALD872B	Arriva London South – Brixton	Iveco	
1873	ES4007	Citybus, Kowloon, Hong Kong (2)	Leyland	rebuilt to vintage open top style
1878	ALD878B	London Borough of Wandsworth (1142)	Leyland	playbus
1882	ALD882B	McDonalds Restaurants, Schongau, Germany	AEC	children's party bus
1883	LIPRM.909	Action Car, Koln, Germany	Leyland	
1885	YBB15167	King Food Corporation (Property) Ltd, Potchefstroom, South Africa	Leyland	
1887	AX32911	Halden Trafikk, Halden, Norway	Leyland	

RM	Registration	Present owner	Engine	Notes
1888	BA4 850	Double Deck Tours (9), Niagara Falls, Ontario, Canada	Leyland	platform doors fitted 2000
1889	16.61	Marchen Japan Co(1), Mito, Japan	Leyland	promotional vehicle, offside emergency exits fitted
1897	GUS594	Staf Cars, Lommel, Belgium	Leyland	
1904	BE9 679	Capital Double Deck & Trolley Tours (11), Ottawa, Ontario, Canada	AEC	
1909	BA4 804	Double Deck Tours (6), Niagara Falls, Ontario, Canada	Leyland	
1911	YSL76B	Anglo European Trade, Budapest, Hungary	AEC	use unknown
1912	ALD912B	Le Grands Pub, Araches (74), France	AEC	converted to British style pub in the French Alps
1913	ALD913B	London Bus Services Ltd	AEC	in storage
1916	ALD913B	Mr C. Learoyd, Altea, near Alicante, Spain	AEC	
1917	ALD917B	Unknown owner, Portoroz, Slovenia	Leyland	condition unknown
1918	ALD918B	King Food Corporation (Property) Ltd, Potchefstroom, South Africa	Leyland	
1919	ALD919B	Arriva Presenting London – Wandsworth	AEC	open top conversion in 1986, Harrods livery
1924	BK4 723	W & G Enterprises, Fulton, Ontario, Canada	AEC	platform door and wheel chair ramp fitted
1930	ALD930B	Cabildo Insular de Lanzarote, Arrecife, Lanzarote, Canary Islands	Leyland	never used since acquisition
1933	ALD933B	London Bus Services Ltd.	AEC	in storage
1936	ALD936B	Blue Triangle, Rainham, Essex	Leyland	in storage
1941	ALD941B	London Bus Services Ltd	AEC	in storage
1943	BB4 951	Capital Double Deck & Trolley Tours (154), Ottawa, Ontario, Canada	Leyland	
1947	ALD947B	Unknown owner, Guststalte Tiechschanke, Geyer, Germany	Leyland	static restaurant with folding canvas high roof
1948	WXA800T	Hator, Warsaw, Poland	AEC	promotional vehicle
1949	ALD949B	Unknown owner, Los Angeles, USA	Leyland	open top, rebuilt with offside exit
1950	BB4 953	Capital Double Deck & Trolley Tours (293), Ottawa, Ontario, Canada	Leyland	open top conversion 1995
1951	ALD951B	94.7FM Concerto, Montevideo, Uruguay	Leyland	open top, used during the Summer time at Punte del Este
1955	ALD955B	London Central – New Cross	Scania	
1959	ALD959B	Marineland Theme Park, Malgrat, Spain	AEC	promotional vehicle
1962	ALD962B	London Central – New Cross	Scania	
1966	ALD966B	McKindless (1950), Wishaw	Leyland	Central Scottish red and cream livery
1968	ALD968B	Mr Sharp, Glasgow	AEC	
1969	ALD969B	Unknown owner, USA	Leyland	wine bar at an unknown location
1971	ALD971B	Metroline – Willesden	AEC	
1975	ALD975B	Mr D Wright, Paisley	Leyland	preserved, named Rory
1977	ALD977B	London Central – New Cross	Scania	
1978	ALD978B	Arriva London South – Brixton	Iveco	
1979	ALD979B	Metroline – Willesden	AEC	
1980	ALD980B	London Central – New Cross	Scania	
1983	PO 17938	London Transport Advertising, Poznán, Poland	AEC	
1986	60 6618	TJW Travels, Fort, Matara, Sri Lanka	AEC	
1988	ALD988B	La Manada Diara Ponet, Lerida, Spain	AEC	
1989	ALD989B	Mr B Lilley, Tilehurst	AEC	preserved, often seen in use with Associated Bus Ministries
1990	ALD990B	Mr S. Bradbury, Reading	AEC	preserved
1991	ALD991B	Antenna Television SA, Maroussi, Athens, Greece	AEC	
1993	ALD993B	Mr P. Durrant, West Ham	Leyland	preserved
2002	EGF299B	City of Collierville, Collierville, Tennessee, USA	AEC	
2003	1NLC88	Senor I. Vargas, Cancun, Mexico	AEC	'Saturday' – courtesy bus for La Boom night club
2005	64 D 805	Dualway Coaches, Rathcoole, Co. Dublin, Ireland	AEC	
2010	AOZ6705	Carlton International Ltd, New Orleans, Lousiana, USA	Leyland	hospitality unit
2011	ALM11B	Mr M. Johnson, Salehurst, Sussex	AEC	Transmatic lighting fitted by Southend Transport

RM	Registration	Present owner	Engine	Notes
2018	ALM18B	Marchen – Japan Co. (2), Mito, Japan	Leyland	promotional vehicle, offside emergency exits fitted
2021	ALM21B	Mr S. Holmes, Blackburn	AEC	preserved
2022	ALM22B	London Central – New Cross	Scania	
2023	ALM23B	RM2097 Group, London	AEC	preserved
2024	PO 06016	London Transport Advertising, Poznán, Poland	AEC	
2026	ALM26B	Koyama Driving School, Kanagawa, Japan	Leyland	waiting room
2032	4123RW47	Societé des Autocars Brouens, Villeneuve sur Lot (47), France	AEC	
2033	ALM33B	London United – Shepherds Bush	AEC	Refurbished by London United in 1997
2037	ALM37B	Mr K Rose, Staines	Leyland	preserved
2041	ALM41B	unknown owner, France	AEC	location and use unknown
2043	ALM43B	Koyama Driving School, Kanagawa, Japan	Leyland	waiting room
2046	SJT736	Parque de la Costa, Tigre, Buenos Aires, Argentina	AEC	
2049	60 6617	Colombo Metropolitan Bus Company Ltd, Sri Lanka – Ratmanlana depot (RL11)	Ashok	
2050	ALM50B	Friends of LT Museum	AEC	at Acton 'Depot'
2051	ALM51B	London Central – New Cross	Scania	
2059	ALM59B	Mr A Haywood, Bromley	Leyland	occasionally loaned to Delaine
2060	ALM60B	London Bus Services Ltd	AEC	in storage, named Rosie
2063	531 647B	Mr S. Levy, Harare, Zimbabwe	AEC	used to transport old age pensioners to a restaurant in Borrowdale village
2065	ALM65B	East Yorkshire (812) – Scarborough	AEC	open top conversion in 1996
2071	ALM71B	London Bus Services Ltd.	AEC	in storage
2077	ALV814	La Plata Patrimonial Cultural de la Humanidad, La Plata, Buenos Aires, Argentina	AEC	
2078	ALM78B	London United – Shepherds Bush	AEC	Refurbished by London United in 1997
2081	EDS620B	F C Sanchez, Rincon de Seca, Murcia, Spain	AEC	use unknown
2087	ALM87B	Anglo European Trade, Budapest, Hungary	AEC	use unknown
2088	60 6638	Gampala Bus Company Ltd, Sri Lanka – Negombo depot (NB106)	Ashok	
2089	ALM89B	London Bus Services Ltd.	Leyland	in storage
2092	60 6616	Colombo Metropolitan Bus Company Ltd., Sri Lanka – Maharagama depot (RL143)	AEC	
2097	ALM97B	RM2097 Group, Hounslow	AEC	preserved
2100	ALM100B	K K B Tarsasag, Szent, Istvan, Hungary	AEC	
2101	ALM101B	McDonalds Restaurants, Apolda, near Weimar, Germany	AEC	children's party bus
2103	ALM103B	Freight Media, Paddington	AEC	promotional vehicle
2106	CUV106C	London Central – New Cross	Scania	refurbished in 2000
2107	CUV107C	International Coachlines, Thornton Heath	Leyland	platform doors fitted in 1999
2109	CUV109C	London Central – New Cross	Scania	refurbished in 2000
2113	CUV113C	MarchenJapan Co, Tokyo, Japan	AEC	promotional vehicle
2114	CUV114C	McDonanld's Restaurants, Budapest, Hungary	AEC	
2116	CUV116C	Messrs G Lunn & T Muir, Egham	AEC	preserved in '1933' livery
2120	HHED 930	last reported with Teleticke GMBH, Hamburg, Germany	AEC	fitted with lightweight lifting roof, current location and use unknown
2121	CUV121C	Mr B. Turner, Bridge of Weir	AEC	preserved
2122	CUV122C	London Bus Services Ltd	AEC	in storage, named Rodney
2124	CUV124C	McDonalds Restaurants, Zoetermere, The Netherlands	AEC	static childrens' party bus
2128	CUV128C	London Central – New Cross	Scania	refurbished in 2000
2129	CUV129C	Freight Media, Paddington	AEC	promotional vehicle
2131	CUV131C	Fukunishi Company Ltd., Osaka, Japan	AEC	location and use unknown
2133	4857XC	Royal Blue Line Motor Tours, Victoria, British Columbia, Canada	AEC	
2136	CUV136C	exported to unknown owner	AEC	location and use unknown

RM	Registration	Present owner	Engine	Notes
2145	CUV145C	Coffee & Beer London Bus, Saitama, Japan	AEC	coffee and beer house
2150	CUV150C	Unknown owner, Tokyo, Japan	AEC	use unknown
2151	CUV151C	London Central – New Cross	Scania	
2152	A1047	Mr M. Overcash, Atlanta, Georgia, USA	AEC	t/a Great Knight Tours, out of use
2153	CUV153C	exported for McDonald's Restaurants	AEC	location unknown, childrens' party bus
2154	CUV154C	Mr J. Gowdy, Ballyclare, Northern Ireland	AEC	preserved
2155	60 6605	Colombo Metropolitan Bus Company Ltd., Sri Lanka – Maharagama depot (MH92)	Ashok	manual gearbox fitted
2156	CUV156C	Nostalgiabus, Mitcham	AEC	
2158	60 6615	Mahanuwara Bus Company Ltd., Sri Lanka – Kandy South depot	AEC	all over advert livery for Mitsui cement
2160	60 6614	Colombo Metropolitan Bus Company Ltd., Sri Lanka – Ratmanlana depot (RL5)	AEC	
2162	BA4 813	Double Deck Tours (14), Niagara Falls, Ontario, Canada	AEC	platform doors fitted 2000
2165	BA4 814	Double Deck Tours (4), Niagara Falls, Ontario, Canada	Leyland	
2166	CUV166C	Sakurai Ham, Kanagawa, Japan	AEC	party bus
2171	CUV171C	Royal Oman Police, Oman	AEC	
2173	CUV173C	Mr M. Walsh, Dunstable	AEC	preserved
2174	HVR007	Mr P. Pesikaka, Tottenham, Ontario, Canada (10)	AEC	t/a London Picadilly Buses
2178	CUV178C	Fuzzy Duzzy Children's Entertainer, Abbots Langley	AEC	
2179	CUV179C	Arriva London South – Brixton	Iveco	
2180	CUV180C	Nostalgiabus, Mitcham	AEC	
2181	CUV181C	British Bus Company, San Diego, California, USA	AEC	open top
2183	23428	Messrs A Rahman & M Taher, Dubai, United Arab Emirates	AEC	
2185	CUV185C	Arriva London North – Clapton	Iveco	refurbished by Leaside in 1997
2186	CUV186C	Quadrini Leisure Group, Newcastle	AEC	used at Tuxedo Princess Night Club
2187	KAG009C	Homegrown, Nairobi, Kenya (T7)	AEC	staff transport
2192	CUV192C	Mr Leonid, Kiev, Ukraine	AEC	playbus
2193	CUV193C	MarchenJapan Co, Tokyo, Japan	AEC	promotional vehicle
2198	CUV198C	Mr M. Drabwell, Bushey	AEC	preserved
2200	6841XA42	Mr A. Oufquim, St. Etienne (42), France	AEC	snack bar
2203	CUV203C	Mac Tours, Cockenzie	AEC	under conversion to open top
2205	CUV205C	S Hori & Partners, Budapest, Hungary	AEC	bar/restaurant
2206	BA4 803	Double Deck Tours (7), Niagara Falls, Ontario, Canada	Leyland	
2207	60 6602	Unknown owner, Greater Colombo, Sri Lanka	AEC	
2208	CUV208C	Mr M. King, Leeds	AEC	preserved in Shillibeer livery
2209	BJ6 943	Double Deck Tours (20), Niagara Falls, Ontario, Canada	AEC	open top
2210	CUV210C	East Yorkshire (816) – Scarborough	AEC	open top conversion in 1996
2212	HHMM278	Hamburger Hummelbahn, Hamburg, Germany	AEC	rebuilt open top with staircase on the left hand side and platform on the right hand side
2213	CUV213C	Mr R. Fletcher, Rahane, Helensburgh	AEC	preserved
2217	CUV217C	Arriva London South – Brixton	Iveco	

RMC	Registration	Present owner	Engine	Notes
4	SLT59	Mr M. Selt, Colchester	Leyland	preserved
1453	453CLT	Arriva London North – Edmonton	AEC	refurbished by Leaside in 1994
1456	LFF875	Stagecoach East London – Upton Park	AEC	refurbished by East London in 1989
1458	115WX29	SARL Crown 3B, Quimper, France	AEC	use unknown
1459	459CLT	Mr P. Almeroth, Wendling, Norfolk	AEC	preserved
1461	461CLT	Stagecoach East London – Upton Park	AEC	Green Line livery, refurbished by East London in 1994
1462	462CLT	Mr J. MacNamara, Raynes Park	AEC	

RMC	Registration	Present owner	Engine	Notes
1464	464CLT	Arriva London North – Edmonton	Iveco	open top conversion in 1990, named Princess
1469	469CLT	Mr K. McGowan, Rotherhithe	AEC	preserved
1474	474CLT	Blue Triangle, Rainham	AEC	in storage
1476	476CLT	Messrs M Knight, Alton & C Warneford, Gillingham	AEC	preserved
1477	477CLT	Mr H. Hobson, Royston	AEC	preserved
1480	PBA541	Gothaelf A.B., Torslanda, Sweden	AEC	promotional vehicle for CocaCola
1481	481CLT	Mr B. Venhofen, Bremerhaven, Germany	AEC	open top
1485	485CLT	Stagecoach East London – Upton Park	AEC	refurbished by East London in 1989
1486	KVS276	Unknown owner, Bad Harzburg, Germany	AEC	use unknown
1487	487CLT	Mr D. Sullivan, Harrow	AEC	preserved
1488	659AQF91	Unknown owner, Essonnes (91), France	AEC	promotional vehicle used for Aids Awareness Campaign
1490	490CLT	Messrs K Kooper, A Haywood & Newton, Bromley	AEC	preserved, Metrobus livery
1492	WXA040W	Mr T. Skrzelinski, Warsaw, Poland	AEC	promotional vehicle
1495	495CLT	Bus Stop Catering, Addlestone	AEC	mobile catering vehicle, named Gus
1496	496CLT	Sextons Hifi, Fulham, London	AEC	promotional vehicle
1497	497CLT	Mr R.C. Gale, Avonwick	AEC	preserved
1499	499CLT	Unknown owner, Argeles-sur-mer (66), France	AEC	accommodation vehicle at Kart Circuit,
1500	ALC368A	Mr P. Hodgson, Romford	AEC	preserved
1503	7806TL56	Herve SARL, Vannes, France	AEC	promotional vehicle at Le Mater Parc du Golfe Leisure complex
1507	507CLT	Mr R. Humphries, Dagenham	AEC	preserved
1510	510CLT	First CentreWest – Westbourne Park	Cummins	open top conversion in 1989, Transmatic lighting fitted to the lower deck in 1993
1513	513CLT	Metroline – Willesden	AEC	refurbished by East London in 1989
1515	515CLT	unknown owner, Galacia, Spain	AEC	open top conversion in 1987, use unknown
1516	516CLT	Mr P. Almeroth, Wendling, Norfolk	AEC	preserved
1519	6005RR13	Mr J.L. Sastre, Marseille, France	AEC	Pizza restaurant

FRM	Registration	Present owner	Engine	Notes
1	KGY4D	London Transport Museum	AEC	at Acton 'Depot', occasional PSV use

RCL	Registration	Present owner	Engine	Notes
2218	CUV218C	London Borough of Redbridge, Goodmayes	AEC	mobile family day centre
2219	CUV219C	BaMMOT, Wythall	AEC	preserved
2220	CUV220C	Arriva Presenting London – Wandsworth	AEC	convertible open top 1991
2221	CUV221C	LRT Central Distribution Services, Acton	AEC	information/exhibition vehicle, available for hire
2223	CUV223C	AVS Graphics Ltd., Stanford-on-Soar	AEC	hospitality vehicle
2226	CUV226C	Aeroshoot Film Services, Hackney	AEC	catering vehicle
2229	CUV229C	London Transport Museum	AEC	at Acton 'Depot'
2233	CUV233C	Mr A Brown, Romford	AEC	preserved
2235	B64416VE	Sr R Tornabell, Sta Eulalia d'Roachz, Barcelona, Spain	AEC	convertible open top 1990, promotional vehicle
2238	CUV238C	Abada Film Services, Leavesden	AEC	catering vehicle
2239	CUV239C	Imperial Buses, Rainham, Essex	AEC	
2240	CUV240C	exported to unknown owner	AEC	convertible open top 1991, location and use unknown
2241	CUV241C	exported to unknown owner	AEC	convertible open top 1991, last reported in overall advert for London Aquarium, location and use unknown
2243	CUV243C	Medway FM, Rochester, Kent	AEC	convertible open top 1990
2245	CUV245C	Eurocermex S.A., Brussels, Belgium	AEC	open top, promoting Corona Extra Beer
2248	CUV248C	Arriva Presenting London – Wandsworth	AEC	convertible open top 1991
2250	CUV250C	Eurocermex S.A., Brussels, Belgium	AEC	open top, promoting Corona Extra Beer
2252	BC8 559	Double Deck Tours (2), Niagara Falls, Ontario, Canada	AEC	platform doors fitted
2253	CUV253C	Mr J Letts, Gillingham, Dorset	AEC	convertible open top 1991, t/a Redbus
2254	CUV254C	Mrs J V Hart, Harrow	AEC	preserved
2255	BC8 555	Double Deck Tours (1), Niagara Falls,		

RMF	Registration	Present owner	Engine	Notes
		Ontario, Canada	AEC	platform doors fitted
2256	CUV256C	Omnibuses Aranjuez S.L., Aranjuez, Spain	AEC	Rebuilt in 1981 with standard RM/RML platform
2259	CUV259C	exported to unknown owner	AEC	convertible open top 1991, location and use unknown
2260	CUV260C	Blue Triangle, Rainham, Essex	AEC	pseudo Green Line livery

RMF/former Northern General vehicles

RMF	Registration	Present owner	Engine	Notes
1254	254CLT	Mr M Biddell, Woodford	AEC	preserved
	RCN689	London Bus Catering, Gothenburg, Sweden	Leyland	Fish & Chip restaurant
	RCN697	Beverage Services, London	Leyland	promotional vehicle currently working for Coca Cola
	PCN762	GoAhead Northern Bus Enthusiasts Association, Gateshead	AEC	preserved (ex RCN699)
	RCN701	International Coachlines, Thornton Heath	Leyland	numbered RMF2771
	EUP405B	Mr D Slater, Newcastle	Leyland	preserved
	GGE986	CreaMobiel, Wommelgem, Belgium	AEC	open top (ex FPT580C)
	FPT581C	Bertie Bus Company, Tewkesbury	Leyland	playbus
	FPT588C	The Big Bus Co, London (RMF 588)	Leyland	open top
	FPT589C	Palladium Disco, Coslada, near Madrid, Spain	Leyland	static advert for discotheque
	FPT590C	Mr G Matthews, Sidcup	AEC	preserved
	FPT591C	London Bus Transport Oy, Espoo, Finland	Leyland	
	FPT592C	The Big Bus Co., London (RMF 592)	AEC	
	FPT603C	The Big Bus Co., London (RMF 603)	Leyland	

RMA/former BEA vehicles
Vehicles are listed in RMA number order (with the former BEA number shown in brackets).

RMA	Registration	Present owner	Engine	Notes
1 (21)	KGJ621D	Mr A. Henderson, Cambridge	AEC	preserved
5 (35)	82-33-LS	Stagecoach Portugal, Cascais, Portugal	AEC	Open top and offside entrance conversion 1997
6 (38)	NMY638E	Mr R. Higgins, Christchurch	AEC	preserved
8 (40)	82-34-LS	Stagecoach Portugal, Cascais, Portugal	AEC	Open top and offside entrance conversion 1997
9 (46)	NMY646E	Mac Tours, Cockenzie	AEC	being prepared for future use
10 (47)	NMY647E	Mr L. Norri, Ikaalinen, Finland	AEC	
11 (48)	NMY648E	Mr K. West, Dagenham	AEC	preserved in Green Rover livery
13 (56)	NMY656E	Mr J.M. Roberts, Kentish Town	AEC	preserved
14 (2)	KGJ602D	Mr P. Graves, Watford	AEC	withdrawn, in storage
15 (11)	KGJ611D	Knihcentrum A S, Prague, Czech Republic	AEC	use unknown
16 (14)	CXX306	Mr J. Carlsson, J C Omnibus, Spångagården, Förslöv, Sweden	AEC	'George the Routemaster' – Clydemaster refurbishment by Clydeside Scottish in 1989
17 (17)	575 LMM 75	Octobus SARL, Paris (75), France	AEC	last reported in '101 Dalmatians' livery
19 (22)	KGJ622D	Mr W. Bullen, Lee, London	AEC	Luxury mobile caravan
20 (33)	4757-WQ-49	Interfoyer du Choletais, Cholet (49), France	AEC	information bus
22 (45)	67 KK 501	J J Kavanagh & Sons Ltd, Urlingford, Co. Kilkenny, Ireland	AEC	
25 (53)	67D813	Dualway Coaches, Rathcoole, Co. Dublin, Ireland	AEC	used to operate Kilkenny Tour, open-top conversion in 1995
26 (60)	67D816	Dualway Coaches, Rathcoole, Co. Dublin, Ireland	AEC	
28 (1)	KGJ601D	Mr J. Stoute, Witton	AEC	preserved
29 (3)	KGJ603D	Mr R. Brown, Motcombe	AEC	rebuilt/lengthened to 32ft long with centre staircase in 1997, numbered as RME1, t/a Shaftesbury & District
37 (12)	KGJ612D	Timebus Travel, St Albans	AEC	
47 (30)	NMY630E	Mr R. Higgins, Christchurch	AEC	preserved, former trainer (i.e. staircase removed)
48 (31)	NMY631E	Blue Triangle, Rainham, Essex	AEC	in storage
49 (32)	NMY632E	Imperial Buses, Rainham, Essex	AEC	
50 (34)	NMY634E	Bluebird Buses (1110) – Lathalmond	AEC	part of Stagecoach preserved fleet

RML	Registration	Present owner	Resident garage	Engine	Notes
880	WLT880	London United (ER880)	Shepherds Bush	Cummins	London United livery
881	HSL656	London United	Shepherds Bush	Cummins	
882	WLT882	Arriva London North	Clapton	Cummins	
883	WLT883	London Central	Camberwell	Cummins	non-opening upper deck front windows
884	WLT884	Arriva London North	Clapton	Cummins	
885	WLT885	First CentreWest	Westbourne Park	Cummins	
886	WLT886	Stagecoach East London	Upton Park	Scania	
887	WLT887	London General	Putney	Iveco	
888	WLT888	Arriva London North	Clapton	Cummins	
889	WLT889	London General	Putney	Iveco	
890	XFF814	Stagecoach East London	Upton Park	Scania	
891	HSL660	London United	Shepherds Bush	Cummins	
892	WLT892	Arriva London South	Brixton	Iveco	
893	KFF276	Metroline	Willesden	Cummins	
894	WLT894	London General	Waterloo	Iveco	
895	WLT895	Arriva London South	Brixton	Iveco	
896	WLT896	Arriva London North	Clapton	Cummins	
897	WLT897	Arriva London North	Clapton	Cummins	
898	XFF813	Stagecoach East London	Bow	Scania	
899	WLT899	London General	Putney	Iveco	
900	WLT900	Blue Triangle, Rainham, Essex		AEC	Clydemaster refurbishment by Clydeside in 1988, undergoing restoration
901	WLT901	Arriva London North	Clapton	Cummins	
902	ALC464A	Metroline	Willesden	Cummins	
903	WLT903	Metroline	Holloway	AEC	
2261	CUV261C	Arriva London North	Tottenham	Cummins	
2262	CUV262C	London General	Waterloo	Iveco	
2263	CUV263C	London General	Waterloo	Iveco	
2264	CUV264C	Arriva London South	Brixton	Iveco	
2265	CUV265C	Sovereign	Edgware	Cummins	
2266	CUV266C	Arriva London South	Battersea	Iveco	
2267	CUV267C	Arriva London North	Tottenham	Cummins	
2268	CUV268C	First CentreWest	Westbourne Park	Cummins	
2269	CUV269C	London United	Shepherds Bush	Cummins	
2270	CUV270C	London Central	Camberwell	Cummins	
2271	CUV271C	London Central	New Cross	Cummins	
2272	CUV272C	Stagecoach East London	Upton Park	Scania	
2273	CUV273C	London Central	Camberwell	Cummins	
2274	CUV274C	Metroline	Willesden	Cummins	
2275	CUV275C	London Central	Camberwell	Cummins	non-opening upper deck front windows
2276	CUV276C	London Central	Camberwell	Cummins	
2277	CUV277C	Arriva London North	Tottenham	Cummins	
2278	CUV278C	First CentreWest	Westbourne Park	Cummins	
2279	CUV279C	London Central	Camberwell	Cummins	
2280	CUV280C	Arriva London North	Clapton	Cummins	
2281	CUV281C	First CentreWest	Westbourne Park	Cummins	
2282	CUV282C	Metroline	Holloway	Cummins	
2283	CUV283C	London Central	New Cross	Cummins	
2284	CUV284C	Metroline	Holloway	Cummins	
2285	CUV285C	Metroline	Willesden	Cummins	
2286	CUV286C	Stagecoach East London	Upton Park	Scania	
2287	CUV287C	Arriva London North	Clapton	Cummins	
2288	CUV288C	Metroline	Willesden	Cummins	
2289	CUV289C	Metroline	Willesden	Cummins	
2290	CUV290C	London General	Putney	Iveco	
2291	CUV291C	First CentreWest	Westbourne Park	Cummins	
2292	CUV292C	Arriva London North	Tottenham	Cummins	
2293	CUV293C	London United	Shepherds Bush	Cummins	
2294	CUV294C	Arriva London North	Tottenham	Cummins	
2295	CUV295C	Metroline	Holloway	Cummins	
2296	CUV296C	Metroline	Holloway	Cummins	
2297	CUV297C	London General	Putney	Iveco	

RML	Registration	Present owner	Resident garage	Engine	Notes
2298	CUV298C	London United	Shepherds Bush	Cummins	
2299	CUV299C	Metroline	Willesden	Cummins	
2300	CUV300C	Stagecoach East London	Bow	Scania	
2301	CUV301C	Arriva London South	Battersea	Iveco	
2302	CUV302C	London Central	Camberwell	Cummins	
2303	CUV303C	Stagecoach East London	Bow	Scania	
2304	CUV304C	Arriva London North	Clapton	Cummins	
2305	CUV305C	London General	Waterloo	Iveco	
2306	??	Mr A Brown, Romford		AEC	preserved
2307	CUV307C	Arriva London South	Brixton	Iveco	
2308	CUV308C	Metroline	Willesden	Cummins	
2309	CUV309C	First CentreWest	Westbourne Park	Cummins	
2310	CUV310C	Metroline	Holloway	Cummins	
2311	CUV311C	Stagecoach East London	Upton Park	Scania	
2312	CUV312C	Metroline	Willesden	Cummins	
2313	CUV313C	First CentreWest	Westbourne Park	Cummins	
2314	CUV314C	London Central	Camberwell	Cummins	
2315	CUV315C	Arriva London North	Tottenham	Cummins	
2316	CUV316C	London General	Putney	Iveco	
2317	CUV317C	London General	Waterloo	Iveco	
2318	CUV318C	London Central	New Cross	Cummins	
2321	CUV321C	London General	Putney	Iveco	
2322	CUV322C	Sovereign	Edgware	Cummins	
2323	CUV323C	Arriva London North	Tottenham	Cummins	
2324	CUV324C	Arriva London South	Brixton	Iveco	
2325	CUV325C	Arriva London North	Clapton	Cummins	
2326	CUV326C	Arriva London North	Clapton	Cummins	
2327	CUV327C	London Central	Camberwell	Cummins	
2328	CUV328C	Arriva London North	Clapton	Cummins	
2329	CUV329C	Arriva London North	Clapton	Cummins	
2330	CUV330C	Arriva London North	Tottenham	Cummins	
2331	CUV331C	Metroline	Willesden	Cummins	
2332	CUV332C	London Central	New Cross	Cummins	
2333	CUV333C	Arriva London South	Brixton	Iveco	
2334	CUV334C	Arriva London North	Clapton	Cummins	
2335	CUV335C	London Central	Camberwell	Cummins	
2336	CUV336C	London Central	Camberwell	Cummins	
2338	CUV338C	London Central	Camberwell	Cummins	
2339	CUV339C	London Central	New Cross	Cummins	
2340	CUV340C	Arriva London North	Tottenham	Cummins	
2341	CUV341C	Sovereign	Edgware	Cummins	
2342	CUV342C	London General	Waterloo	Iveco	
2343	CUV343C	Arriva London South	Battersea	Iveco	
2344	CUV344C	Arriva London North	Clapton	Cummins	
2345	CUV345C	London Central	New Cross	Cummins	
2346	CUV346C	Arriva London North	Tottenham	Cummins	
2347	CUV347C	Arriva London South	Battersea	Iveco	
2348	CUV348C	Metroline	Willesden	Cummins	
2349	CUV349C	London United	Shepherds Bush	Cummins	
2350	CUV350C	Arriva London North	Tottenham	Cummins	
2351	CUV351C	Arriva London South	Brixton	Iveco	
2352	CUV352C	First CentreWest	Westbourne Park	Cummins	
2353	CUV353C	London United	Shepherds Bush	Cummins	
2354	CUV354C	Arriva London North	Clapton	Cummins	
2355	CUV355C	Arriva London North	Clapton	Cummins	
2356	CUV356C	Arriva London North	Clapton	Cummins	
2357	CUV357C	First CentreWest	Westbourne Park	Cummins	
2358	CUV358C	London General	Waterloo	Iveco	
2359	CUV359C	Arriva London North	Clapton	Cummins	
2360	CUV360C	London General	Waterloo	Iveco	
2361	CUV361C	London General	Putney	Iveco	
2362	CUV362C	London Central	Camberwell	Cummins	

RML	Registration	Present owner	Resident garage	Engine	Notes
2363	CUV363C	London General	Waterloo	Iveco	
2364	JJD364D	London General	Putney	Iveco	
2365	JJD365D	First CentreWest	Westbourne Park	Cummins	
2366	JJD366D	Arriva London South	Brixton	Iveco	
2367	JJD367D	Metroline	Holloway	Cummins	
2368	JJD368D	Metroline	Willesden	Cummins	
2369	JJD369D	First CentreWest	Westbourne Park	Cummins	
2370	JJD370D	Arriva London North	Clapton	Cummins	
2371	JJD371D	London General	Putney	Iveco	
2372	JJD372D	Arriva London North	Tottenham	Cummins	
2373	JJD373D	Arriva London North	Tottenham	Cummins	
2374	JJD374D	First CentreWest	Westbourne Park	Cummins	
2375	JJD375D	Arriva London South	Brixton	Iveco	
2376	JJD376D	London General	Putney	Iveco	
2377	JJD377D	Metroline	Willesden	Cummins	
2378	JJD378D	First CentreWest	Westbourne Park	Cummins	
2379	JJD379D	First CentreWest	Westbourne Park	Cummins	
2380	JJD380D	Arriva London North	Tottenham	Cummins	
2381	JJD381D	London Central	Camberwell	Cummins	
2382	JJD382D	Arriva London South	Battersea	Iveco	
2383	JJD383D	Arriva London South	Battersea	Iveco	
2384	JJD384D	Metroline	Willesden	Cummins	
2385	JJD385D	London General	Waterloo	Iveco	
2386	JJD386D	Arriva London North	Clapton	Cummins	
2387	JJD387D	Arriva London South	Battersea	Iveco	
2388	JJD388D	First CentreWest	Westbourne Park	Cummins	
2389	JJD389D	London General	Waterloo	Iveco	
2390	JJD390D	First CentreWest	Westbourne Park	Cummins	
2391	JJD391D	Arriva London North	Tottenham	Cummins	
2392	JJD392D	Stagecoach East London	Bow	Scania	
2393	JJD393D	Metroline	Holloway	Cummins	
2394	JJD394D	Arriva London North	Tottenham	Cummins	
2395	JJD395D	Metroline	Holloway	Cummins	
2396	JJD396D	London Central	Camberwell	Cummins	
2397	JJD397D	London Central	Camberwell	Cummins	
2398	JJD398D	London General	Putney	Iveco	
2399	JJD399D	Stagecoach East London	Bow	Scania	
2400	JJD400D	London Central	Camberwell	Cummins	
2401	JJD401D	Arriva London North	Clapton	Cummins	
2402	JJD402D	Stagecoach East London	Bow	Scania	
2403	JJD403D	London General	Waterloo	Iveco	
2404	JJD404D	Sovereign	Edgware	Cummins	
2405	JJD405D	First CentreWest	Westbourne Park	Cummins	
2406	JJD406D	Arriva London North	Clapton	Cummins	
2407	JJD407D	Arriva London South	Brixton	Iveco	
2408	JJD408D	Arriva London North	Tottenham	Cummins	
2409	JJD409D	Arriva London North	Clapton	Cummins	
2410	JJD410D	Arriva London South	Battersea	Iveco	
2411	JJD411D	London Central	Camberwell	Cummins	
2412	JJD412D	London General	Putney	Iveco	
2413	JJD413D	Metroline	Holloway	Cummins	
2414	JJD414D	London United	Shepherds Bush	Cummins	
2415	JJD415D	Stagecoach East London	Bow	Scania	
2416	JJD416D	Arriva London North	Clapton	Cummins	
2418	JJD418D	Arriva London North	Tottenham	Cummins	
2419	JJD419D	Metroline	Holloway	Cummins	
2422	JJD422D	London General	Putney	Iveco	
2428	JJD428D	First CentreWest	Westbourne Park	Cummins	
2429	JJD429D	Stagecoach East London	Bow	Scania	
2430	JJD430D	Metroline	Willesden	Cummins	
2431	JJD431D	Metroline	Willesden	Cummins	
2432	JJD432D	London United	Shepherds Bush	Cummins	

RML	Registration	Present owner	Resident garage	Engine	Notes
2434	JJD434D	Arriva London North	Tottenham	Cummins	
2435	JJD435D	Stagecoach East London	Bow	Scania	
2437	JJD437D	Stagecoach East London	Bow	Scania	
2439	JJD439D	Metroline	Willesden	Cummins	
2440	JJD440D	London Central	Camberwell	Cummins	
2441	JJD441D	London General	Putney	Iveco	
2442	JJD442D	First CentreWest	Westbourne Park	Cummins	
2443	JJD443D	Metroline	Holloway	Cummins	
2444	JJD444D	Stagecoach East London	Bow	Scania	
2445	JJD445D	Stagecoach East London	Upton Park	Scania	
2446	JJD446D	Metroline	Willesden	Cummins	
2447	JJD447D	London United	Shepherds Bush	Cummins	
2450	JJD450D	Stagecoach East London	Bow	Scania	
2451	JJD451D	Stagecoach East London	Bow	Scania	
2452	JJD452D	Arriva London South	Battersea	Iveco	
2453	JJD453D	London General	Putney	Iveco	
2454	JJD454D	London Central	Camberwell	Cummins	
2455	JJD455D	London United	Shepherds Bush	Cummins	
2456	JJD456D	Stagecoach East London	Upton Park	Scania	
2457	JJD457D	Arriva London North	Clapton	Cummins	
2460	JJD460D	Arriva London North	Tottenham	Cummins	
2461	JJD461D	London General	Putney	Iveco	
2462	JJD462D	Stagecoach East London	Bow	Scania	
2463	JJD463D	London United	Shepherds Bush	Cummins	
2464	JJD464D	London United	Shepherds Bush	Cummins	
2465	JJD465D	London General	Waterloo	Iveco	
2466	JJD466D	London General	Putney	Iveco	
2467	JJD467D	First CentreWest	Westbourne Park	Cummins	
2468	JJD468D	Arriva London North	Tottenham	Cummins	
2469	JJD469D	London Central	Camberwell	Cummins	
2470	JJD470D	Stagecoach East London	Bow	Scania	
2471	JJD471D	Metroline	Willesden	Cummins	Allison MT643 gearbox fitted
2472	JJD472D	London General	Putney	Iveco	
2473	JJD473D	First CentreWest	Westbourne Park	Cummins	
2474	JJD474D	London Central	Camberwell	Cummins	
2475	JJD475D	London General	Putney	Iveco	
2476	JJD476D	First CentreWest	Westbourne Park	Cummins	
2477	JJD477D	Arriva London South	Brixton	Iveco	
2478	JJD478D	Metroline	Willesden	Cummins	
2479	JJD479D	Metroline	Holloway	Cummins	
2480	JJD480D	First CentreWest	Westbourne Park	Cummins	
2481	JJD481D	Stagecoach East London	Bow	Scania	
2482	JJD482D	London Central	Camberwell	Cummins	
2483	JJD483D	Arriva London North	Clapton	Cummins	
2484	JJD484D	London Central	Camberwell	Cummins	
2485	JJD485D	London United	Shepherds Bush	Cummins	
2486	JJD486D	First CentreWest	Westbourne Park	Cummins	
2487	JJD487D	Sovereign	Edgware	Cummins	
2488	JJD488D	Stagecoach East London	Bow	Scania	
2489	JJD489D	London United	Shepherds Bush	Cummins	
2490	JJD490D	First CentreWest	Westbourne Park	Cummins	
2491	JJD491D	Arriva London South	Brixton	Iveco	
2492	JJD492D	Arriva London North	Clapton	Cummins	
2493	JJD493D	Stagecoach East London	Bow	Scania	
2494	JJD494D	Arriva London North	Clapton	Cummins	
2495	JJD495D	Stagecoach East London	Upton Park	Scania	
2496	JJD496D	Stagecoach East London	Upton Park	Scania	
2497	JJD497D	Stagecoach East London	Upton Park	Scania	
2498	JJD498D	First CentreWest	Westbourne Park	Cummins	
2499	JJD499D	London Central	Camberwell	Cummins	
2500	JJD500D	London United	Shepherds Bush	Cummins	
2501	JJD501D	First CentreWest	Westbourne Park	Cummins	

RML	Registration	Present owner	Resident garage	Engine	Notes
2502	JJD502D	London General	Putney	Iveco	
2503	JJD503D	Arriva London North	Tottenham	Cummins	
2504	JJD504D	Arriva London North	Tottenham	Cummins	
2505	JJD505D	Arriva London South	Battersea	Iveco	
2506	JJD506D	First CentreWest	Westbourne Park	Cummins	
2507	JJD507D	London Central	New Cross	Cummins	
2508	JJD508D	Metroline	Willesden	Cummins	
2509	JJD509D	Metroline	Willesden	Cummins	
2510	JJD510D	Arriva London North	Tottenham	Cummins	
2511	JJD511D	Metroline	Holloway	Cummins	
2512	JJD512D	Arriva London South	Battersea	Iveco	
2513	JJD513D	London Central	Camberwell	Cummins	
2514	JJD514D	Arriva London South	Battersea	Iveco	
2515	JJD515D	London Central	Camberwell	Cummins	
2516	WLT516	London General	Waterloo	Iveco	platform doors fitted and reclassified DRM in 1991
2517	JJD517D	London General	Waterloo	Iveco	
2518	JJD518D	Arriva London North	Tottenham	Cummins	
2519	JJD519D	London United	Shepherds Bush	Cummins	
2520	JJD520D	London General	Putney	Iveco	
2521	JJD521D	Arriva London South	Brixton	Iveco	
2522	JJD522D	First CentreWest	Westbourne Park	Cummins	
2523	JJD523D	Arriva London South	Battersea	Iveco	
2524	JJD524D	Arriva London South	Battersea	Iveco	
2525	JJD525D	Arriva London North	Tottenham	Cummins	
2526	JJD526D	Arriva London North	Clapton	Cummins	
2527	JJD527D	Sovereign	Edgware	Cummins	
2528	JJD528D	Arriva London North	Tottenham	Cummins	
2529	JJD529D	London Central	Camberwell	Cummins	
2530	JJD530D	First CentreWest	Westbourne Park	Cummins	
2531	JJD531D	Arriva London South	Battersea	Iveco	non-opening upper deck front windows
2532	JJD532D	Metroline	Willesden	Cummins	
2533	JJD533D	Arriva London South	Battersea	Iveco	
2534	JJD534D	Arriva London North	Clapton	Cummins	
2535	JJD535D	London General	Putney	Iveco	
2536	JJD536D	Arriva London South	Battersea	Iveco	
2537	JJD537D	Metroline	Willesden	Cummins	
2538	JJD538D	Sovereign	Edgware	Cummins	
2539	JJD539D	London Central	New Cross	Cummins	
2540	JJD540D	London General	Putney	Iveco	
2541	JJD541D	Stagecoach East London	Upton Park	Scania	
2542	JJD542D	First CentreWest	Westbourne Park	Cummins	
2543	JJD543D	London General	Putney	Iveco	
2544	JJD544D	Arriva London North	Tottenham	Cummins	new offside illuminated advert panels fitted upon refurbishment in 1992
2545	JJD545D	Arriva London South	Brixton	Iveco	
2546	JJD546D	Arriva London North	Tottenham	Cummins	
2547	JJD547D	Metroline	Willesden	Cummins	
2548	JJD548D	Arriva London South	Battersea	Iveco	
2549	JJD549D	Arriva London South	Brixton	Iveco	
2550	JJD550D	Stagecoach East London	Upton Park	Scania	
2551	JJD551D	London Central	Camberwell	Cummins	
2552	JJD552D	Arriva London North	Clapton	Cummins	
2553	JJD553D	First CentreWest	Westbourne Park	Cummins	
2554	JJD554D	London Central	Camberwell	Cummins	
2555	JJD555D	First CentreWest	Westbourne Park	Cummins	
2556	JJD556D	London Central	Camberwell	Cummins	
2558	JJD558D	Metroline	Willesden	Cummins	
2559	JJD559D	First CentreWest	Westbourne Park	Cummins	
2560	JJD560D	London Central	Camberwell	Cummins	
2561	JJD561D	Metroline	Holloway	Cummins	
2562	JJD562D	Arriva London North	Tottenham	Cummins	

RML	Registration	Present owner	Resident garage	Engine	Notes
2563	JJD563D	Sovereign	Edgware	Cummins	
2564	JJD564D	London General	Putney	Iveco	
2565	JJD565D	Stagecoach East London	Upton Park	Scania	
2566	JJD566D	Metroline	Willesden	Cummins	
2567	JJD567D	Arriva London North	Clapton	Cummins	
2568	JJD568D	London General	Putney	Iveco	
2569	JJD569D	Sovereign	Edgware	Cummins	
2570	JJD570D	London General	Putney	Iveco	
2571	JJD571D	Arriva London North	Tottenham	Cummins	
2572	JJD572D	Arriva London South	Brixton	Iveco	
2573	JJD573D	Arriva London South	Brixton	Iveco	
2574	JJD574D	Arriva London South	Battersea	Iveco	
2575	JJD575D	London General	Putney	Iveco	
2576	JJD576D	London General	Putney	Iveco	
2577	JJD577D	Arriva London South	Battersea	Iveco	
2578	JJD578D	London Central	New Cross	Cummins	
2579	JJD579D	Metroline	Willesden	Cummins	
2580	JJD580D	London General	Putney	Iveco	
2581	JJD581D	Stagecoach East London	Upton Park	Scania	
2582	JJD582D	Sovereign	Edgware	Cummins	
2583	JJD583D	London Central	New Cross	Cummins	
2584	JJD584D	London Central	New Cross	Cummins	
2585	JJD585D	Metroline	Willesden	Cummins	
2586	JJD586D	Arriva London South	Battersea	Iveco	
2587	JJD587D	London Central	Camberwell	Cummins	
2588	JJD588D	Arriva London North	Tottenham	Cummins	new offside illuminated advert panels fitted upon refurbishment in 1992
2589	JJD589D	Arriva London North	Tottenham	Cummins	
2590	JJD590D	London General	Putney	Iveco	
2591	JJD591D	Arriva London South	Battersea	Iveco	
2592	JJD592D	Stagecoach East London	Bow	Scania	
2593	JJD593D	London General	Putney	Iveco	
2594	JJD594D	Metroline	Willesden	Cummins	
2595	JJD595D	Arriva London North	Tottenham	Cummins	
2596	JJD596D	London Central	New Cross	Cummins	
2597	JJD597D	Arriva London North	Clapton	Cummins	
2598	JJD598D	Sovereign	Edgware	Cummins	
2599	NML599E	Metroline	Willesden	Cummins	
2600	NML600E	London United	Shepherds Bush	Cummins	
2601	NML601E	London Central	Camberwell	Cummins	
2602	NML602E	First CentreWest	Westbourne Park	Cummins	
2603	NML603E	Metroline	Holloway	Cummins	
2604	NML604E	London Central	New Cross	Cummins	
2605	NML605E	London General	Putney	Iveco	
2606	NML606E	London General	Waterloo	Iveco	
2607	NML607E	Stagecoach East London	Bow	Scania	
2608	NML608E	Arriva London South	Brixton	Iveco	
2609	NML609E	First CentreWest	Westbourne Park	Cummins	
2610	NML610E	Stagecoach East London	Upton Park	Scania	
2611	NML611E	Arriva London North	Tottenham	Cummins	
2612	NML612E	London General	Putney	Iveco	
2613	NML613E	London Central	New Cross	Cummins	
2614	NML614E	London Central	Camberwell	Cummins	
2615	NML615E	London General	Putney	Iveco	
2616	NML616E	Stagecoach East London	Upton Park	Scania	
2617	NML617E	Arriva London North	Tottenham	Cummins	
2618	NML618E	London General	Waterloo	Turbocharged Iveco	
2619	NML619E	Arriva London South	Battersea	Iveco	
2620	NML620E	Metroline	Holloway	Cummins	
2621	NML621E	London United	Shepherds Bush	Cummins	
2622	NML622E	London United	Shepherds Bush	Cummins	
2623	NML623E	First CentreWest	Westbourne Park	Cummins	

RML	Registration	Present owner	Resident garage	Engine	Notes
2624	NML624E	Stagecoach East London	Bow	Scania	
2625	NML625E	Arriva London North	Tottenham	Cummins	
2626	NML626E	London General	Putney	Iveco	
2627	NML627E	Sovereign	Edgware	Cummins	
2628	NML628E	Arriva London North	Tottenham	Cummins	
2629	NML629E	London Central	Camberwell	Cummins	
2630	NML630E	London Central	Camberwell	Cummins	
2631	NML631E	London General	Putney	Iveco	
2632	NML632E	Arriva London North	Tottenham	Cummins	
2633	NML633E	Metroline	Holloway	Cummins	
2634	NML634E	Metroline	Willesden	Cummins	
2635	NML635E	Arriva London North	Tottenham	Cummins	
2636	NML636E	Arriva London South	Brixton	Iveco	
2637	NML637E	London General	Putney	Iveco	
2638	NML638E	Arriva London North	Tottenham	Cummins	
2639	NML639E	Stagecoach East London	Upton Park	Scania	
2640	NML640E	London General	Putney	Iveco	
2641	NML641E	Stagecoach East London	Upton Park	Scania	
2642	NML642E	Stagecoach East London	Upton Park	Scania	
2643	NML643E	Arriva London North	Tottenham	Cummins	
2644	NML644E	London General	Putney	Iveco	
2645	NML645E	London United	Shepherds Bush	Cummins	
2646	NML646E	London United	Shepherds Bush	Cummins	
2647	NML647E	First CentreWest	Westbourne Park	Cummins	
2648	NML648E	London General	Waterloo	Iveco	
2649	NML649E	Metroline	Willesden	Cummins	
2650	NML650E	London United	Shepherds Bush	Cummins	
2651	NML651E	Metroline	Willesden	Cummins	
2652	NML652E	Metroline	Willesden	Cummins	
2653	NML653E	Arriva London South	Brixton	Iveco	
2654	NML654E	London General	Putney	Iveco	
2655	NML655E	Arriva London North	Tottenham	Cummins	
2656	NML656E	First CentreWest	Westbourne Park	Cummins	
2657	NML657E	Stagecoach East London	Bow	Scania	
2658	SMK658F	Arriva London North	Tottenham	Cummins	
2659	SMK659F	Metroline	Holloway	Cummins	
2660	SMK660F	Arriva London North	Tottenham	Cummins	
2661	SMK661F	Stagecoach East London	Upton Park	Scania	
2662	SMK662F	London United	Shepherds Bush	Cummins	
2663	SMK663F	Sovereign	Edgware	Cummins	
2664	SMK664F	First CentreWest	Westbourne Park	Cummins	
2665	SMK665F	Stagecoach East London	Bow	Scania	
2666	SML666F	Arriva London North	Tottenham	Cummins	
2667	SMK667F	First CentreWest	Westbourne Park	Cummins	
2668	SMK668F	Sovereign	Edgware	Cummins	
2669	SMK669F	London General	Waterloo	Iveco	
2670	SMK670F	Stagecoach East London	Upton Park	Scania	
2671	SMK671F	Stagecoach East London	Upton Park	Scania	
2672	SMK672F	First CentreWest	Westbourne Park	Cummins	
2673	SMK673F	London Central	New Cross	Cummins	
2674	SMK674F	Sovereign	Edgware	Cummins	
2675	SMK675F	Arriva London North	Clapton	Cummins	
2676	SMK676F	London Central	Camberwell	Cummins	
2677	SMK677F	First CentreWest	Westbourne Park	Cummins	
2678	SMK678F	Arriva London North	Tottenham	Cummins	
2679	SMK679F	Metroline	Holloway	Cummins	
2680	SMK680F	London General	Waterloo	Iveco	
2681	SMK681F	Metroline	Willesden	Cummins	
2682	SMK682F	Arriva London North	Clapton	Cummins	
2683	SMK683F	London Central	Camberwell	Cummins	
2684	SMK684F	Arriva London North	Tottenham	Cummins	
2685	SMK685F	Arriva London North	Clapton	Cummins	

RML	Registration	Present owner	Resident garage	Engine	Notes
2686	SMK686F	Sovereign	Edgware	Cummins	
2687	SMK687F	First CentreWest	Westbourne Park	Cummins	
2688	SMK688F	Arriva London North	Clapton	Cummins	
2689	SMK689F	Metroline	Willesden	Cummins	
2690	SMK690F	Metroline	Willesden	Cummins	
2691	–	Big Bengt Erlandsson, High Chapperal, Hillerstorp, Sweden		AEC	
2692	SMK692F	Arriva London South	Brixton	Iveco	
2693	SMK693F	London General	Waterloo	Iveco	
2694	SMK694F	Sovereign	Edgware	Cummins	
2695	SMK695F	Metroline	Willesden	Cummins	
2696	SMK696F	Stagecoach East London	Bow	Scania	
2697	SMK697F	London United	Shepherds Bush	Cummins	
2698	SMK698F	Metroline	Willesden	Cummins	
2699	SMK699F	Metroline	Holloway	Cummins	
2700	SMK700F	London United	Shepherds Bush	Cummins	
2701	SMK701F	Metroline	Willesden	Cummins	
2702	SMK702F	London United	Shepherds Bush	Cummins	
2703	SMK703F	Metroline	Willesden	Cummins	
2704	SMK704F	London United	Shepherds Bush	Cummins	
2705	SMK705F	Stagecoach East London	Upton Park	Scania	
2706	SMK706F	Metroline	Willesden	Cummins	
2707	SMK707F	London United	Shepherds Bush	Cummins	
2708	SMK708F	Arriva London North	Tottenham	Cummins	
2709	SMK709F	Stagecoach East London	Bow	Scania	
2710	SMK710F	Metroline	Willesden	Cummins	
2711	SMK711F	London Central	Camberwell	Cummins	
2712	SMK712F	London Central	Camberwell	Cummins	
2713	SMK713F	Metroline	Willesden	Cummins	
2714	SMK714F	London Central	Camberwell	Cummins	
2715	SMK715F	Arriva London South	Battersea	Iveco	
2716	SMK716F	Arriva London North	Clapton	Cummins	
2717	SMK717F	First CentreWest	Westbourne Park	Cummins	
2718	SMK718F	Arriva London South	Brixton	Iveco	
2719	SMK719F	Sovereign	Edgware	Cummins	
2720	SMK720F	London United	Shepherds Bush	Cummins	
2721	SMK721F	London United	Shepherds Bush	Cummins	
2722	SMK722F	London United	Shepherds Bush	Cummins	
2723	SMK723F	Stagecoach East London	Upton Park	Scania	
2724	SMK724F	First CentreWest	Westbourne Park	Cummins	
2725	SMK725F	London General	Waterloo	Iveco	
2726	SMK725F	Arriva London South	Brixton	Iveco	
2727	SMK727F	Metroline	Willesden	Cummins	
2728	SMK728F	Metroline	Willesden	Cummins	
2729	SMK729F	London United	Shepherds Bush	Cummins	
2730	SMK730F	Arriva London South	Brixton	Iveco	
2731	SMK731F	Metroline	Holloway	Cummins	
2732	SMK732F	London General	Waterloo	Iveco	
2733	SMK733F	London Central	Camberwell	Cummins	
2734	SMK734F	London United	Shepherds Bush	Cummins	
2735	SMK735F	First CentreWest	Westbourne Park	Cummins	
2736	SMK736F	London General	Waterloo	Iveco	
2737	SMK737F	Metroline	Willesden	Cummins	
2738	SMK738F	Stagecoach East London	Bow	Scania	
2739	SMK739F	London United	Shepherds Bush	Cummins	
2740	SMK740F	First CentreWest	Westbourne Park	Cummins	
2741	SMK741F	Arriva London South	Brixton	Iveco	
2742	SMK742F	Arriva London North	Tottenham	Cummins	
2743	SMK743F	Stagecoach East London	Upton Park	Scania	
2744	SMK744F	London United	Shepherds Bush	Cummins	
2745	SMK745F	London General	Putney	Iveco	air brakes fitted in 1992
2746	SMK746F	Arriva London North	Tottenham	Cummins	

RML	Registration	Present owner	Resident garage	Engine	Notes
2747	SMK747F	Arriva London North	Tottenham	Cummins	
2748	SMK748F	Stagecoach East London	Upton Park	Scania	
2749	SMK749F	Stagecoach East London	Bow	Scania	
2750	SMK750F	Arriva London North	Clapton	Cummins	
2751	SMK751F	London United	Shepherds Bush	Cummins	
2752	SMK752F	London General	Waterloo	Iveco	
2753	SMK753F	Arriva London South	Brixton	Iveco	
2754	SMK754F	Arriva London North	Clapton	Cummins	
2755	SMK755F	Metroline	Willesden	Cummins	
2756	SMK756F	Sovereign	Edgware	Cummins	
2757	SMK757F	London United	Shepherds Bush	Cummins	
2758	SMK758F	Arriva London North	Clapton	Cummins	
2759	SMK759F	Arriva London South	Brixton	Iveco	
2760	SMK760F	Stagecoach East London	Upton Park	AEC	traditional style refurbishment in 1990

ROUTEMASTER TYPES
RM:RML:RMC:RCL:RMA:RMF:FRM

Sub-frames:	AEC Routemaster model	R2RH	– all RM/RMC vehicles
		R2RH/1	– RML 2261–2760
		R2RH/3	– RCL 2218–2260
		R2RH/2	– RMA 1–65
		2R2RH	– all RM vehicles originally fitted with Leyland units
		3R2RH	– RMF 1254 and former Northern General vehicles
		FR2R	– FRM

Engine:	AEC	AV590 9.6 litre developing 115bhp at 1800 rpm
	AEC	AV690 11.3 litre developing 175 bhp at 2200 rpm
	AEC	AV691 11.3 litre developing 150 bhp at 1800 rpm (FRM)
	Leyland	600 9.8 litre developing 150 bhp at 1800 rpm
	Iveco	83611 8.1 litre rated at MW at 1800 rpm
	Cummins	6C8 8.27 litre rated at 112kW at 2200 rpm
	Cummins	B series 5.9 litre rates at 145 bhp at 2500 rpm
	DAF	DK1 160VS 11.6 litre rated at 145 bhp at 1800 rpm
	Scania	DS9 9.6 litre

Bodywork: Park Royal (seating and layout as below), or
LTE/PRV (RM 1 and 2), or
Weymann (RM 3), or
Eastern Coach Works (RMC 4).

Built:			Number built:	
RM	1954/5/7–1965			2123
RMA	1966–1967		65	
RMC	1957, 1962		69	
RMF	1964/5			51
RML	1962/1965–1968			524
RCL	1965			43
FRM	1966			1
		Total		**2876**

Classifications:		
	RM	Standard Routemaster.
	RMA	Front entrance Routemaster (ex British Airways).
	RMC	Routemaster Coach (ex Green Line).
	RML	Routemaster lengthened.
	RMF	Front entrance Routemaster lengthened (ex Northern General).
	RME	Routemaster Extended (former RMA).
	RCL	Routemaster Coach Lengthened (ex Green Line).
	ER	Extended Routemaster (RML).
	ERM	Extended Open Top Routemaster (RM).
	DRM	RML fitted with RMC rear end + doors.
	FRM	Front entrance Routemaster (rear engine).

LONDON OPERATORS

Route	Terminals	Garage	Operation	PVR	Operator	End of current contract
6	Aldwych to Kensal Rise Station	Willesden	Mon-Sat	22	Metroline	12/12/03
7	Russell Square to East Acton Station	Westbourne Park	Mon-Sat	13	First CentreWest	23/6/05
8	Victoria Station to Bow Church	Bow	Mon-Sat*	25	Stagecoach East London	26/6/04
9	Hammersmith Bus Stn to Aldwych	Shepherds Bush	Mon-Sat	17	London United	4/9/04
10	Hammersmith Bus Stn to Archway Stn	Holloway	Mon-Sat	23	Metroline	21/8/04
11	Liverpool Street Stn to Fulham Bdy	Waterloo	Mon-Fri	20	London General	27/6/03
12	Notting Hill Gate to Dulwich Plough	Camberwell	Mon-Sat	38	London Central	24/7/04
13	Golders Green Station to Aldwych	Edgware	Mon-Sat	18	Sovereign	17/8/00
14	Putney Heath to Tottenham Court Road Stn	Putney	Mon-Sat	22	London General	13/9/02
15	Paddington Station to East Ham	Upton Park	Mon-Sat	24	Stagecoach East London	22/8/03
19	Finsbury Park Stn to Battersea Bridge	Battersea	Mon-Sat	18	Arriva London South	28/4/05
22	Putney Common to Piccadilly Circus	Putney	Mon-Sat	15	London General	21/7/05
23	Liverpool St Stn to Westbourne Park Stn	Westbourne Park	Mon-Sat	29	First CentreWest	22/8/03
36	Queens Park Station to Lewisham	New Cross	Mon-Sat	44	London Central	26/5/05
38	Victoria Station to Clapton Pond	Clapton	Mon-Sat	41	Arriva London North	19/7/02
73	Victoria Stn to Stoke Newington Common	Tottenham	Mon-Sat	48	Arriva London North	1/5/04
94	Acton Green to Piccadilly Circus	Shepherds Bush	Mon-Sat	22	London United	17/10/03
98	Willesden to Holborn, Red Lion Square	Willesden	Mon-Sat	21	Metroline	12/12/03
137	Streatham Hill to Oxford Circus	Brixton	Mon-Sat	25	Arriva London South	18/9/04
159	Marble Arch to Streatham	Brixton	Mon-Sat	24	Arriva London South	28/1/06

* On Sundays a number of RMLs operate on route 8.

Operator	Total pvr	No. in stock
Arriva London North	89	105
Arriva South London	67	78
First CentreWest	42	49
London Central	82	97
London General	57	69
London United	39	41
Metroline	66	80
Sovereign	18	19
Stagecoach East London	49	62
Totals	**509**	**600**

REGISTRATION INDEX

(for vehicles in the United Kingdom only)

Registration number	Vehicle number
CJS 112	RM 804.
DSL 540	RM 1033.
HSI 656, 660	RML 881, 891.
HVS 935	RM 255.
JFO 256	RM 23.
JSJ 743, 767, 797.	RM 1260, 872, 1174.
JSJ 746–749.	ERM 90, 84, 80, 94.
KFF 239, 257, 276, 367	RM 659, 646, RML 893, RM 1101.
KVS 599, 601	RM 408, 471.
LFF 875	RMC 1456.
LSL 827	RM 966.
MFF 509, 578, 580	RM 1312, 329, 931.
NVS 485	RM 1292.
OVS 940	RM 875.
PCN 762	ex NGT 2099.
PVS 828, 830	RM 1018, 1020.
RCN 689, 697, 701	ex NGT 2089, 2097, 2101.
RSK 572	RM 110.
RSL 259	RM 1590.
SLT 56–59	RM 1–3, RMC 4.
SSL 806, 809	RM 121, 120.
SVS 617, 618	RM 432, 548.
USK 625	RM 980.
UYJ 654	RM 1224.
VLT 5–9, 16, 24, 25, 40, 44, 66, 70, 85, 108, 111, 116, 140, 158, 188, 196, 200, 202, 216, 238, 254, 259, 268, 275, 291, 295	RM 5 etc.
VLT 143, 163, 235, 237, 242, 281	ERM 143, 163, 235, 237, 242, 281.
VVS 373	RM 125.
VYJ 806, 808, 876	RM 1124, 1361, 1262.
WFO 410	RM 378.
WLT 307, 308, 316, 324, 348, 349, 371, 376, 385, 428, 436, 446, 450, 460, 478, 506, 529, 531, 541, 545, 577, 581, 597, 613, 642, 644, 652, 654, 655, 664, 676, 687, 710, 719, 737, 742, 752, 753, 758, 759, 765, 782, 787, 795, 811, 822, 835, 848, 857, 871, 912, 928, 938, 960, 967, 970, 991, 994, 997	RM 307 etc.
WLT 516	DRM 2516.
WLT 675	RM 17.
WLT 875	RM 666.
WLT 880	ER 880.
WLT 882–889	RML 882–889.
WLT 892	RML 892.
WLT 894–897	RML 894–897.
WLT 899–901	RML 899–901.
WLT 903	RML 903.
WSJ 737, 739.	RM 479, 313.
WVS 423	RM 999.
XFF 258, 813, 814	RM 10, RML 898, 890.
XVS 828, 830, 839, 850, 851	RM 843, 180, 244, 1083, 467.
XYJ 418, 427, 440	RM 736, 1185, 838.
YVS 288, 294	RM 357, 229.
71 AWN	RM 1397.
100 BXL	RM 1000.
1, 3, 9, 58, 62, 63, 69, 82, 97, 104, 119, 123, 138, 152, 159, 168, 204, 214, 218, 280, 305, 321, 324, 348, 353, 357, 363, 368, 380, 394, 403, 414, 449, 527, 543, 562, 563, 571, 583, 593 CLT	RM 1001 etc.

Registration number	Vehicle number
254 CLT	RMF 1254.
453, 459, 461, 462, 464, 469, 474, 476, 477, 485, 487, 490, 495, 496, 497, 507, 510, 513, 515, 516 CLT	RMC 1453 etc.
627, 640, 641, 643, 650, 654, 677, 691, 699, 725, 734, 735, 737, 747, 767, 771, 776, 783, 797, 799, 801, 822, 840, 859, 864 DYE	RM 1627 etc.
ALC 290, 368, 464A	RM 1005, RMC 1500, RML 902.
AST 415, 416A	RM 45, 191.
BNK 324A	RM 1568.
EDS 50, 221, 288, 300, 320A	RM 560, 1010, 910, 388, 606.
KGH 858, 975A	RM 1125, 1330.
KGJ 117, 118, 142, 187, 339, 341A	RM 1528, 1398, 311, 1621, 1400, 1666.
LDS 67, 164, 201, 210, 236, 238, 239, 279, 282, 341, 402A	RM 1274, 978, 1607, 1245, 272, 697, 727, 54, 245, 441, 1145.
NSG 636A	RM I 164.
OYM 368, 424, 453A	RM 1002, 14, 29.
WTS 245, 418A	RM 298, 909.
XMD 81A	RM 429.
XSL 596A	RM 1289.
YTS 820A	RM 1599
ALD 871, 872, 878, 913, 919, 933, 936, 941, 955, 962, 966, 968, 971, 975, 977, 978, 979, 980, 989, 990, 993B	RM 1871 etc.
ALM 11, 21, 22, 23, 33, 37, 50, 51, 59, 60, 65, 71, 78, 89, 97, 103B	RM 2011 etc.
BFW 544B	RM 1842.
EGF 220, 285B	RM 1811, 1836.
EVM 132B	RM 1807.
EUP 405B	ex NGT 2105.
EYY 327B	RM 1804.
CUV 106, 107, 109, 116, 121, 122, 128, 151, 154, 156, 173, 178, 179, 180, 185, 186, 198, 203, 208, 210, 213, 217C	RM 2106 etc.
CUV 218–221, 223, 226, 229, 233, 238–241, 243, 248, 253, 254, 259, 260C	RCL 2218 etc.
CUV 261–305C	RML 2261–2305.
CUV 307–318C	RML 2307–2318.
CUV 321–336C	RML 2321–2336.
CUV 338–363C	RML 2338–2363.
FPT 581, 588, 590, 592, 603C	ex NGT 2111, 2118, 2120, 2122, 2133.
KGY 601–603, 612, 621, 622D	RMA 28, 14, 29, 37, 1, 19.
JJD 364–416D	RML 2364–2416.
JJD 418, 419, 422D	RML 2418, 2419, 2422.
JJD 428–432D	RML 2428–2432.
JJD 434, 435, 437D	RML 2434, 2435, 2437.
JJD 439–447D	RML 2439–2447.
JJD 450–457D	RML 2450–2457.
JJD 460–556D	RML 2460–2556.
JJD 558–598D	RML 2558–2598.
KGY 4D	FRM 1.
NML 599–657E	RML 2599–2657.
NMY 630, 631, 632, 634, 637, 638, 641, 644, 646, 648, 654, 655, 656, 662, 665E	RMA 47, 48, 49, 50, 52, 6, 53, 55, 9, 11, 57, 58, 13, 62, 65.
SMK 658–69OF	RML 2658–2690.
SMK 692–76OF	RML 2692–2760.